ON THE BOUNDARY

On the Boundary

A VISION FOR
NON-STIPENDIARY MINISTRY

by

ROD HACKING

With a Foreword by

BISHOP GEORGE CAREY

The Canterbury Press
Norwich

First published 1990 by The Canterbury Press Norwich
(a publishing imprint of Hymns Ancient & Modern Limited)
St Mary's Works, St Mary's Plain,
Norwich, Norfolk, NR3 3BH

British Library Cataloguing in Publication Data
Hacking, Rod
On the boundary.
1. Church of England. Non-stipendiary clergy
I. Title
262.143

ISBN 1-85311-014-0

*Typeset by Rowland Phototypesetting Limited
Bury St Edmunds, Suffolk
and printed in Great Britain by
St Edmundsbury Press Limited
Bury St Edmunds, Suffolk*

*Dedicated
to the staff and students of
S.D.M.T.S.*

ERRATUM
Page 89. In the table of figures, for year 1988
under column headed "% Women of Total",
please read 30.2 for 43.3.

FOREWORD

I accepted Rod Hacking's invitation to write this Foreword because I am wholeheartedly committed to the ministry of non-stipendiary clergy. I have plenty of evidence of this form of ministry operating well in my diocese and the qualities of care, dedication and love of God exercised by many of these men and women are truly exemplary. I don't need convincing of the value of the non-stipendiary minister.

But while I am committed to it, I am also very concerned that over the last ten years or so it seems that we have lost our way a little. There is confusion about whether the ministry should be work-based or church-based, there has been some confusion about the identity of non-stipendiary ministry, leading to a steady trickle of people shifting into stipendiary ministry; there has been apathy on the part of some leaders, incumbents and lay people to affirm and support the ministry of the non-stipendiary disciple.

For both of these reasons I am delighted that Rod Hacking has written this most helpful book. He does so rooted in the training of non-stipendiary clergy in a Course and College which has pioneered new forms of training. And the book is written in such a way that it is accessible to the person not trained to handle erudite theology. Warm, witty and intelligent *On the Boundary* will make an important contribution to the ongoing debate about Christian ministry today.

+ George Bath & Wells

ACKNOWLEDGEMENTS

To the following publishers I am grateful for permission to quote copyright material: SCM Press, SPCK, SVS Press and CUP.

I also wish to record my thanks to the many students and non-stipendiary ministers who have been willing to share with me something of their experience and in particular the Revv. Kate Pryde, Margaret Venables, Christine Sindall, Alan Viller and David Spencer.

My colleague Dr David Way kindly provided some help with biblical material and Alistair Redfern made helpful comments on the manuscript for which I am grateful. Canon John Fuller worked very hard indeed on an early draft of the book and has helped me avoid a number of pitfalls, though he is in no way responsible for what remains.

I would like to thank Bishop George Carey for agreeing to write a foreword and to Kenneth Baker of The Canterbury Press Norwich for his friendship and support.

As always my chief debt is to my family who patiently bear having to share me with a word processor and constantly offering their loving support.

March 1990   RH

CONTENTS

Foreword   vii

Introduction: In the Shadow of the Spire   1

1. Between the Past and the Present   7

2. Between Clergy and Lay   28

3. Between the Church and the Kingdom of God   56

4. Between Men and Women   85

5. Between the Christian and the Human   102

6. Between the Present and the Future   134

For Further Reading   150

In the Shadow of the Spire

The Close in Salisbury is an interesting and remarkably appropriate place in which to think about the ordained ministry of the Church. At its heart stands the Spire, quintessentially English and beloved of Constable, Turner and the hordes of American and French tourists who flock in homage every day. At the time of writing (and probably for some years to come) it is curiously shrouded in scaffolding and reminds me of Dean Jocelin's construction, a symbol of manhood and God, forever pointing to a reality greater than itself. William Golding, erstwhile master at the Grammar School adjacent to where now I work, chose his symbol well, for the spire at Salisbury is etched deep in the unconscious of all whose nostalgia is for a golden religious past. It is a reminder too, that in the late medieval period this was a place of great importance, the home of 'Sarum' liturgical usage which exercised a considerable hold upon the worship of the Church in this country up to the time of the first Prayer Book of 1549. The Cathedral and Close of Salisbury has had, and continues to have, a powerful hold upon the mind of the Church in England in one way or another.

Another figure whose existence is etched deep within the unconscious of countless men and women of England is George Herbert, who for three years was rector of the nearby parish of Bemerton, and who was indeed ordained priest beneath the spire. According to Isaac Walton, twice each week Herbert walked the couple of miles or so across the water meadows to play his lute or viol within the confines of the Close. Although Herbert had already written his *Country Parson* before he came to Bemerton, his brief ministry there has somehow seemed the ideal of what pastoral ministry in the Church of England is all about. When a friend of mine was recently interviewed for a parochial appointment of which the patrons were the Dean and Chapter of a Cathedral he was asked about his models for ministry. He responded with the name of Herbert, and one can only assume from the fact he was appointed to the particular benefice that there are still senior clerics in the Church of England who believe that far-off romantic vision enshrined in classical seventeenth century prose provides the foundations for an urban ministry at the end of the twentieth century. But the waters of Herbert's vision run deep within the Anglican soul; I may feel dismay but not surprise.

Another figure whose vision of England runs deep within the heart of the English is Anthony Trollope. Each day I trace the course of his own daily journey across Harnham Bridge, past St Nicholas' Hospital and into the Close through the Harnham Gate. The 'hospital' is actually an almshouse, model for Hiram's Hospital, home to the Reverend Septimus Harding, the Warden, and father-in-law to Archdeacon Grantly. The ghosts of Dr and Mrs Proudie and the detestable Obadiah Slope can still be seen about the place, or perhaps they are not ghosts at all but their successors within this strange world which is locked and bolted at 11 pm each day. At one end of the Close dwells the Bishop, at the other, the Dean, and in between a former Prime Minister and Canons in their green cassocks. How Trollopian too, that during 1989 a major controversy in the life of the Close and Cathedral has centred upon plans to construct toilets for visitors, a construction which would only be visible from the air! Given the storm of feeling engendered by such plans (and it has threatened to turn the Close into an English Clochemerle), one might be forgiven for feeling that nothing of substance has changed here for generations. It is a feeling further enhanced by the constant refrain of Choral Evensong 'as it was in the beginning, is now and ever shall be'. To look around is almost to believe not only that God is in his heaven, but that all is well within the Church, and that it, like Him, is unchanging. So When Susan Howatch came to write the first three of her recent set of novels on the twentieth century Church of England, not only does the Close (barely disguised) figure prominently within them but she actually came into the Close to do the writing. Where else?

It is within the Close, under the afternoon shadow of the spire that I now work. In a way of course it is an obvious setting for a Theological College, with all these powerful images near at hand. My own theological college was within sight and sound of the cathedral of Canterbury and it is not surprising that a good number of others have had close associations with the mother churches of their respective dioceses. However things are not always as they appear even within the Close at Salisbury.

The theological college now houses two institutions, making it the largest centre for training men and women for the ordained ministry of the Church of England with almost 150 ordinands. Salisbury and Wells Theological College came into being in 1971 after the College at Wells closed, joining forces with students here, a college dating back to 1864. Although by far the more ancient institution, in terms of student numbers it is in fact marginally the smaller. The younger and larger is the Southern Dioceses Ministerial Training Scheme (SDMTS), which began in 1974.

The difference between the two lies in the style of training offered. The College trains men and women in a residential context, whereas the Course does so largely non-residentially. Employed by one and with a significant teaching role in the other provides me with both an interesting view of the nature and shape of the process of ministerial formation as well as a vision of the sort of Church and ministry for which we seem to be preparing men and women today. As this book is much concerned with the boundaries between various groups and ideas, this particular institution is a first boundary, between different styles of training, and a place of encounter, between people preparing for ministry in different ways and sometimes for different styles of ministry. Most of those preparing for ordination in the College will be hoping to go on to stipendiary ministry in a parish. Most, but by no means all, of those preparing on the Course, are hoping to go on to exercise a non-stipendiary ministry.

The temptation for residential students to be swallowed up by the Close and its spectres is great though mercifully most manage to survive it. For the non-residential students, who come here for just five weekends and an eight-day Summer School each year, it is all quite different. They mostly arrive here on a Friday evening direct from their work-place or the realities of their day to day existence. Some come from the world of industry, some from schools where they teach, some from hospitals or surgeries, others come from running a home and managing complex family arrangements. They bring with them the pressures and complexities of a busy week and as they drive under the arch of the North Gate into the Close it is as if they are entering another world altogether. No doubt for some it is a happy escape, a weekend away from the compromises and pressures, a chance to look forward to the ministry to which they feel called, but most do not see it that way.

SDMTS students, like all other Anglicans, recognise the imagery of the past and its powerful pull in the present, but coming from their particular place in the world they do sometimes wonder whether this rarified environment and all it represents has anything whatsoever to do with what lies beyond its walls, both literal and metaphorical.

For their teachers too, a recognition of the circumstances in which these students have to do both their training and their theology, means that we cannot but root theology differently from the highly rarified context in which many of us first learned it in university departments. So this corner of the Close is for me a boundary between the theology we learn and teach and the realities of human life. It is not about something that belongs to a closed world, akin to Calvin's Institutes, a perfectly rounded system flawed only by its total unreality.

Increasingly I have come to see that theology needs to be done on the boundaries, because that is where theology encounters reality, its temper tested and flaws revealed. It is there too that the ordained minister belongs. My own experience as an ordained minister, whether as a parish priest or as an industrial chaplain has shown me again and again that clergy are marginal people anyway, but that far from being a cause of lamentation we should see this as a strength, and that being willing to stand on the margins, on the boundaries without having recourse to the securities of the past, is precisely the place where we should be willing to stand. If the ordained minister really is a representative person, both of Christ and the Church, then she and he need to accept that in Christ we follow a marginal person, someone crucified outside the city walls not in the temple, and that what characterises the Church is not standing still but, like fire, spreading outwards.

This book is concerned with exploring the possibilities and hopes that non-stipendiary ministry can embody and express. Of course such aspirations may be shared by stipendiary ministers too, but, as I shall attempt to show, it is particularly with the non-stipendiary minister that some of these hopes may be realised. Equally I am clear that not every non-stipendiary minister or student in training, will want to share them. There are no doubt many men and women choosing non-stipendiary ministry to evade reality not face it even more rigorously. It is however about possibility and a hope for the Church and, even more, for the Kingdom of God.

It is very much a personal vision, written in the hope that it might 'ring bells' with others engaged in or giving thought to the possibility of non-stipendiary ministry. Although a recent report *Called to Order* expresses the hope that the

Church of England will continue to rely heavily upon stipendiary ministry it is nevertheless abundantly clear that non-stipendiary ministry in some form or other is going to be more and more important. A great deal of thought is now being given, nationally and locally, as to the best means of preparing men and women for this ministry. Plans are being drawn up for the reorganisation of training courses and various dioceses are setting up imaginative schemes for the further development of 'local' non-stipendiary ministry. Just what form or content these schemes may have is yet to emerge and I can recognise in some of them dangers that they will end up being more 'churchy' than I would hope. I am seeking to draw on my own, albeit limited, experience of ministry in diverse contexts together with the experience of a good number of others engaged in non-stipendiary ministry or in training such ministers in the hope that some NSMs at least will see the possibilities engendered by their ordination as the means toward a larger vision.

In chapter five I describe the impact made upon the ministry of NSMs following the decision of the Church of England to admit women to the order of deacon. At the present time more women than men are coming forward for ordination as non-stipendiary ministers. For that reason, together with the principle of positive discrimination, wherever appropriate (i.e. not when referring to still all-male ministries) I have used feminine pronouns to refer to NSMs in general, though men are of course included. Living on that particular boundary is, I am convinced, both uncomfortable and necessary.

CHAPTER ONE

Between the Past and the Present

Non-stipendiary ministry was a long time coming. Or perhaps, we should say, it was a long time reappearing, for it could be said that it was the original model for ministry, at least in so far as the New Testament is concerned.

Luke informs us that Jesus and his disciples were supported by a number of women during the course of his ministry (Lk. 8.3). Contemporary rabbis could expect to be kept by their disciples and supporters and Jesus' style of operation seems to accord well with current practice, though one rabbinic school in particular, that of Gamaliel, seems to have encouraged its students to learn and practice a trade by which to support themselves if need be. Though teachers such as Jesus might well extol the virtues of living by simple faith and trust (c.f. Matthew 6.25–33) the fact of his women supporters and the homes in which he and his disciples were clearly welcomed reveals a necessary practicality about him.

In sending out the disciples, whether the twelve or the seventy-two, Jesus seems to have insisted that they exercise considerable discernment in seeking out the most likely places and people of support to accompany their otherwise basic lifestyle (Matt. 10.5–14). The expectation seems clear, that his agents had the right to be kept by others as did he.

Within the earliest community in Jerusalem after the resurrection, it seems pretty certain that the group of apostles maintained a similar pattern. The pooling of resources enabled the maintenance of the distinctive pattern of life of the apostles. Later, when the system of support within the Jerusalem church broke down under the impact of persecution and famine the principle was extended well beyond the boundaries of Israel (c.f. 1 Cor. 16,1.1–3 or 2 Cor. 8 & 9).

The first of the apostles to exercise a different kind of approach to financial support was Paul, who had of course been trained as a rabbi under Gamaliel. It is therefore quite likely that Paul had undertaken an apprenticeship in tent making (though the Greek word has more often been used to refer to a saddler or leather worker) during his time in the school of his famous teacher.

During the years after his conversion and before he began his missionary work it is more than likely that Paul maintained himself through the practice of his trade. In later years too he clearly used this trade to support himself both as he journeyed and also during his prolonged stays in different communities (Acts 18.3; 1 Thess. 2.9; 1 Cor. 4.12; 2 Cor. 11.27). He may of course have had no choice. We know that there was considerable controversy about whether or not Paul really was an apostle, and in spite of his protestations it may well be that Paul was not wholly successful in convincing all the communities in which he ministered that he had the right to be supported by them, as the other apostles apparently did. Not that he himself doubted the right, even if, as he reminded the Corinthians, it was something he chose not to claim (1 Cor. 9.1–15). Instead, staying in the home of Aquila and his wife Priscilla, he worked with them in their leather business. It would have been a brave person however who would have dared to suggest that Paul was not a full-time minister!

In addition to the apostles there were a considerable number of other ministries within the early church. The lists in 1 Cor. 12.28, Ephesians 4.11 and 1 Tim. 3 & 4 name at least eleven others and there is no evidence whatsoever to suggest that those holding these offices were released from the necessities of employment in order to fulfil their demands. Paul often refers to the local leaders of the communities where he worked as his 'fellow-workers' (Rom.

16.3; 1 Thess. 3.2). Just as in Romans 16.3–5 Paul refers to his fellow leather-workers Prisca and Aquila as his 'fellow workers' in the work of the gospel, so we can assume that in almost all cases the local ministers of the Church were not set apart from the demands of having to earn their daily bread, no matter in what other way they were set apart for their particular ministries.

Just how long these patterns of ministry were maintained is unclear. The emergence of the pattern of bishop, presbyter and deacon seems to have been well-established by the end of the first century, but whether or not these were paid or maintained positions is not clear. It seems likely that those engaged in a presbyteral ministry (sometimes described by the term *episkopoi* – suggesting that the later differentiation between priest and bishop had not yet been made) had an itinerant ministry for which they would have had to rely on the support of the communities they served. Other ministers, including the deacons and other leaders (who eventually became the presbyters of a later period) were almost certainly not acting as paid functionaries. It is clear from the New Testament that the exercise of ministry within the Church does not preclude the possibility that the minister may engage in a secular occupation.

As time went on, and especially after the conversion of Constantine at the beginning of the fourth century (which changed the Church from being a persecuted and minority sect into the official, established Church of the Roman Empire), the clergy began to acquire considerable power, prestige and a secure social position which no longer necessitated manual labour, though Patrick Vaughan (in *Working for the Kingdom* pp. 117–188) has shown that at least in the late Patristic period, clerics, including the occasional bishop, could still be found fulfilling their vocation whilst simultaneously engaged in secular employment.

In subsequent years the Church grew in pecuniary and political power and the activities of clergy were increasingly circumscribed by the expansion of canon law. Even so, by the time of the Reformation there were many abuses among the clergy to which the reformers had to give their attention. One of the earliest attempts appears in the Pluralities Act of 1529, by which clergy were expressly forbidden engagement in activities that could be construed as trade or dealing in goods or merchandise, the penalty for which would be suspension of loss of benefice income (though notably absent from the proscribed activities were teaching in a school or other seat of learning, publishing or farming of a limited kind, in which activities there is clear evidence that many clergy were to engage in subsequent years).

The Ordinal of the 1549 Prayer Book, the first official book of the reformed Church in England, was clearly an attempt, not merely to set out a different understanding of ministry to that which preceded it, but also to correct abuse, among which was clearly the experience of ordained ministers engaging in 'secular' occupations. Henceforth the Bishop was to charge his ordinands to set aside worldly cares and study, applying themselves instead 'wholly to this one thing'. Such an injunction was to be backed up in the major revision of Canon Law completed in 1604 which threatened excommunication to any ordained person engaging in 'base or servile labour' or otherwise behaving like a layman.

The first challenge to the provisions of the Pluralities Act was made in 1841 by Thomas Arnold, formerly Headmaster of Rugby School, newly-apointed Regius Professor of Modern History at Oxford, and father of the poet Matthew Arnold. He had already made a name for himself as a Church reformer and vigorous opponent of the Tractarians who sought, as he saw it, to imprison the Church in an enhanced ecclesiasticism. Perhaps under the impetus of the Methodist pattern of local preachers Arnold wrote a pamphlet arguing for the ordination of working men as deacons. The grounds of his argument were that there was going to be a shortage of clergy, especially in urban areas, which this would alleviate, as well as helping to bridge what he considered to be a false distinction between clergy and laity. Arnold maintained that his proposals were in fact not violating any principle of Church life, merely adapting custom. He was unable to pursue his ideas further for he died in 1842 and for the next forty years the Church was far too distracted by the controversies associated with the development of the Oxford movement to attend to the sort of radical proposals he had been advancing.

The protagonists of the high church party were wanting to emphasise the special and distinctive nature of the ordained ministry not diminish its significance by extending it to include working men. One of their number, William Bright, Regius Professor of Ecclesiastical History at Oxford (and author of the well-known hymn 'And now O father, mindful of thy love') expressed the view in 1887, when a further attempt was made in the Convocation of Canterbury to press for the ordination of working men as deacons, that the evidence from the early church did not permit such a departure from tradition. Not that convocation needed such historical persuasion. There was a considerable strength of opinion that ordination was a 'profession' and to a gathering of such professional gentlemen, the idea of a man holding two such 'professions' seemed self-evidently contradictory.

It is interesting to note that the next phase of momentum towards the ordination of non-stipendiary ministers arose out of experiences gained in the mission fields, experiences often quite different from those who know only the life of the Church of England. Roland Allen had worked as a missionary in northern China before returning to England as an incumbent in Buckinghamshire. He had already argued for changes in the practice of leadership and authority in the Church, but in 1923 he published a key work *Voluntary Clergy*. There had been a significant drop in the number of clergy in the immediate post-war years and as early as 1919 there had been requests from the Diocesan Conferences of London and Southwark for a reconsideration of the theological premises currently barring clergy from holding secular employment. In this context Allen's proposals were to be highly influential.

He maintained that it was quite unjustifiable that people in remote areas should be denied the sacraments merely because of a shortage of a professional clergy. He therefore proposed that following what he believed was apostolic precedence, the natural, respected and mature leaders of a local community be ordained as what he called 'voluntary' clergy.

His ideas won a small measure of support among the bishops at home and abroad with whom he engaged in private correspondence, sufficient to prompt the Church Assembly in 1929 to request an official report on the possibility of voluntary clergy. However such hopes that Allen entertained of the imminence of change were to be dashed when the Bishops of the 1930 Lambeth Conference felt unable to give it their support. The effect of this was to curtail the Church Assembly's exploration of the subject. As in former years the predominant feeling was that priesthood was a profession of which no one could undertake more than one at once, though it is notable that one of the main arguments used against change was that lay people in particular were opposed to it. Bishop Winnington-Ingram of London recounted that having allowed laymen to administer the chalice in certain instances, he had received a considerable amount of opposition to his move, not from clergy but from other laity who felt that they 'did not want to see somebody in that position on Sunday when they were going to do business with them on Monday'. It seems that his argument won the day.

The first moves towards real change began in 1945 in an appended note to the Church Assembly Report *Towards the Conversion of England*. The note came from a subcommittee chaired by Mervyn Stockwood, the vicar of St Matthew, Moorfields, in Bristol, and made two recommendations:

'In some circumstances, a parish priest should be allowed to take a job in industry for a shorter or longer period. In exceptional circumstances, an industrial worker should be ordained as a deacon or priest, to remain in industry and exercise his ministry as an industrial worker.'

In fact these recommendations were not acted upon, most of the attention of the appended note being placed on the emerging ministry of 'factory chaplains'. This had arisen out of the experience of Ted Wickham who in 1944 had been appointed by Bishop Leslie Hunter of Sheffield as diocesan missioner to industry, following pioneering work in munitions factories earlier in the war. During the following years Industrial Mission was increasingly to be seen as the principal focus of the Church's attempts to relate to the world of work.

Another development which would eventually have significant consequences for the development of non-stipendiary ministry was the massive work of Canon Law Reform carried out from 1939 onwards. The committee appointed to look into the questions arising from Canon 83 – 'Of the manner of Life of Ministers' (and which included among its numbers Mervyn Stockwood, by now Vicar of Great St Mary's, Cambridge – the University Church) reported in 1955. It outlined three principal reasons for change in favour of allowing clergy to hold secular occupations:

(a) that declining numbers of clergy made a supplementary parish ministry essential;
(b) that men already exercising roles of pastoral responsibility in the secular world would be that much more effective if they were ordained;
(c) that this would be a key way of bridging what it recognised as a gap dividing the life of the Church from the realities of industrial life.

Consequently the report pressed the cause of a revised canon which would 'not exclude any development along the line of a supplementary ministry'.

The committee set out practical ideas as to how such a ministry might develop. In particular they sought to clarify just how this new style of ministry would relate to the traditional patterns of parochial life, at that stage the only model with which they had to work. It was, they stressed:

'. . . essential that the character and function of these alternative ministries should be thought out, at the outset, without continual reference to the extent to which they can supplement the work of the parish priest.'

It would be important, they maintained, that such ministers be regarded not merely as unpaid curates, and, in suggesting that they be answerable directly to their licensing bishop, assumed that they would have the right to deal with such pastoral matters as came to them in the course of their secular activities without recourse to a local incumbent, even though, for reasons of mutual support, they suggested that every such minister should be attached to a parish.

Convocation received and discussed the report over three separate sessions accepting the need for a revised canon but referring back the matter of supplementary ministry for further consideration. In 1959 the revised canons appeared, the wording of the appropriate passage being as follows:

'No minister holding ecclesiastical office shall engage in trade or any other occupation, except so far as he be authorised so to do under the statutory provisions in this behalf for the time being in force or he have a licence so to do granted by the bishop of the diocese.'

By now there were movements elsewhere which were to have significant consequences for the practice of the Church of England. The first was emergent publicity being given to the worker-priest movement in France. From 1942 a number of those being trained at the seminary at Lisieux were being sent, as part of their training, into heavily industrialised areas, where the traditional Church had all but collapsed. Following on from this experience Cardinal Suhard freed a small number of priests from their parochial roles to move more freely among workers and establish Christian communities. In 1944 one priest, Camille Folliet, went a step further and enlisted as a worker in a big factory, an example which a number of others followed in the ensuing years. By 1954 there were about 100 worker priests including seven Belgians. However at this stage Pope Pius XII intervened through the papal nuncio in Paris, Mgr Marella (who, the previous year, had replaced Mgr Roncalli on his appointment as Patriarch of Venice – later Pope John XXIII), and terminated the worker-priest 'experiment'. Although the experiment was partially to be restored after Vatican 2, in the 1950s Rome was at least successful in putting a stop to what it saw as something essentially dangerous, but what it could not stop was a widespread approval of the movement both within the wider Roman Church and other denominations beyond.

A second element which contributed to eventual change was the Lambeth Conference of 1958. The diocese of Hong Kong, under the leadership of its remarkable and far-sighted bishop, R. O. Hall, had already begun ordaining non-stipendiary clergy (it had also been the first a decade earlier to ordain a woman). Other oriental churches were similarly committed whilst at home there was heavy-weight support for the idea from Archbishop Michael Ramsey of York and Bishop Russell Barry of Southwell, though the latter had been a keen protagonist for many years.

During the first war Barry had served as a forces chaplain and gone on from 1919 to 1923 to serve as Principal of the Knutsford Ordination School which dealt especially with men returning from the front, and where he had, among others, 'Tubby' Clayton, the founder of Toc-H, on his staff. Thereafter he had worked as a Professor at Kings College, London and Vicar of the University Church in Oxford, before returning to London 1933 to spend his time, before becoming Bishop of Southwell in 1941, as a Canon of

Westminster. Whilst there he had written a book *The Relevance of the Church* in which he had pressed the case for what he called the 'non-stipendiary ministry' (though it is not clear whether we can actually say he invented the term or derived it from the writings of Roland Allen). Now almost twenty-five years later, this widely-respected bishop was once again arguing in its favour, arguments which received further support from the appearance of a new book edited by Robin Denniston *Part Time Priests?*, a collection of essays in which the arguments for change were generally stronger than those against.

The third element which contributed to eventual change was the opening on 16 September 1960, of the Southwark Ordination Course (SOC). Once again the influence of Mervyn Stockwood was determinative. In 1959 Harold Macmillan had appointed him Bishop of Southwark, and almost his first act was to appoint (and very much against the wishes of Archbishop Fisher) a former curate from his time in Bristol, now a highly regarded biblical scholar at Cambridge, John Robinson, as Bishop of Woolwich. Together they enabled a radical departure from all previous patterns of training. The part-time training pattern established by SOC was eventually to be normative for training for the non-stipendiary ministry, though it must be remembered that in its earliest years SOC was primarily training men for the stipendiary ministry.

Mervyn Stockwood was never one to worry over much about what his fellow bishops thought of him and from the earliest days he was allowing some of those trained on SOC to remain in their secular jobs after ordination, anticipating (and perhaps thereby enabling) the eventual changes agreed by the church as a whole following the appearance in 1968 of the report *A Supporting Ministry* (more usually known as the 'Welsby Report'). By this time at least one other diocese, Gloucester, had followed the example of Southwark and set up its own training scheme and it is hard to escape the feeling that the Welsby Report was an example of the

Church Assembly officially claiming as its own a band-wagon that was already rolling.

The recommendations of the report were turned into precise resolutions of the Assembly and accepted in 1970 in the form of *Bishops' Regulations for the Selection and Training of Candidates for Auxiliary Pastoral Ministries.* In the following ten years more than 800 men would be ordained as non-stipendiary ministers. Meanwhile, back in the mid-'60s, a GP, Dr Una Kroll, became the first woman student of SOC, preparing for ministry as a deaconess. In 1985 out of a course entry of 21 students with the Southern Dioceses Ministerial Training Scheme, women students preparing for ordination were, for the first time, in the majority.

By 1982 there were already fifteen courses offering training for ordination to the non-stipendiary ministry, in addition to which a small number of experiments have been begun in what has been called 'local non-stipendiary ministry', the earliest being that which involved seven men ordained deacon in 1972 by the Bishop of Stepney, Trevor Huddleston. Initially the emphasis of this was on ordaining men in and from working-class backgrounds (by far the majority of other non-stipendiary candidates coming from middle-class occupations). A number of dioceses have now begun exploring the possibilities of local non-stipendiary ministry, with an emphasis much more on practical skills acquired locally, i.e. in the parish, rather than on the academic requirements still required by, what is now, the traditional NSM training pattern. In most dioceses considerably more thought is currently being given to the pattern of training for the whole church, lay and ordained. One of the features of the years since the inception of non-stipendiary ministry has been a rediscovery of a variety of ministries and ministers, not just the professional clergy, and future developments in local non-stipendiary ministry will no doubt be set firmly within the overall context of thinking about this.

With more than twenty-five years of experience and approaching something near fifteen hundred ordained ministers, the NSM begins to feel a well -established part of the life of the Church. The table following shows the extent to which the number of ordinations to the NSM has grown as a proportion of all ordinations, so that throughout the past fifteen years it has been constantly in the region of a fifth to a quarter:

Year	Ordained	NSMs	NSM % of Total
1971	405	12	3.0
1972	359	19	5.3
1973	372	22	6.0
1974	384	38	9.9
1975	373	52	14.0
1976	357	76	21.3
1977	380	79	20.8
1978	387	80	20.7
1979	406	103	25.4
1980	414	103	24.9
1981	434	123	28.3
1982	425	112	26.3
1983	460	119	25.9
1984	422	109	25.8
1985	406	102	25.1
1986	413	87†	21.1

(Figures supplied by ACCM. † includes some local NSMs)

During these years different patterns of non-stipendiary ministry have begun to play more of a part in the life of other churches too. In the Church in Wales, for example, nearly ten per cent of the clergy by the early 1980s were NSMs. In the Scottish Episcopal Church the numbers have been much smaller but already the practice is well-established. Across the Atlantic there is a group called NASSAM (National Association for the Self Supporting Active Ministry) which claims that twenty per cent of active Episcopalian clergy are non-stipendiary, engaged in a 'Tentmaker Ministry', as some of their published material describes it (though perhaps somewhat cynically one might observe that most of them seem to be engaged in a form of tentmaking which offers a very high financial return!).

Other denominations too have begun experimenting with forms of non-stipendiary ministry. Within the Roman Catholic Church there are now considerable numbers of 'permanent deacons', often older married men, who continue to earn their living or live on their state pension, and who practice a mainly liturgical and pastoral role in the life of the local church. Within the United Reformed Church there is now an Association of Ministers in Secular Employment, and although numbers are still small, and training is mainly done through Anglican courses, the auxiliary ministry (for both men and women) is beginning to be an established feature of URC life. Although the Methodist Conference in 1977 accepted the recommendations of a working party which supported it, the Methodist Church has been much slower to accept what it calls the Sector Ordained Ministry. In the main this has been a result of a continuing debate within the church about the nature of ordination. Even so there are currently about 135 such ministers operating within the Methodist Church, and a further number in training.

It has been said that it is probably easier to convince a pick-pocket to earn his living in a nudist colony than to convince the church of a radical innovation! Certainly in practice it can take the churches a very long time for ideas to become change. The process whereby the churches have begun to take seriously the need for, and now the ministries of, non-stipendiary ministers has been long. In the end it has happened less because the worth of the idea has suddenly been realised than because there have been major changes in society and the world as a whole which have often thrown the churches into a fair degree of turmoil. Some of the response to this turmoil has been little more than a largely unsuccessful re-packaging of the original product (some would suggest, for example, that this is how the ASB should be regarded). In other cases however, and among them I would want to include the development of the NSM within the overall context of a rethinking of ministry, there have been important attempts made at discovering ways in which the Church, whilst remaining true to the catholic and apostolic faith of its foundations, can genuinely be renewed and strengthened for mission in a new age.

Yet after twenty-five years there is still a surprising amount of ignorance within the Church at every level, including the episcopal, of just what non-stipendiary ministry is. Most NSMs have become used to being described as 'part-time' or their ministry as something they do in their 'spare time', and there are unquestionably a good many stipendiary clergy who have a considerable degree of suspicion and scepticism about these people whom they sometimes accuse of having come into ministry 'by the back door'.

As simply as possible, non-stipendiary ministers are those who seek, without any remuneration from the Church, to exercise a full-time ministry to which they have been ordained by the Church, often whilst continuing in their 'secular' jobs. They may well be non-stipendiary (i.e. they don't get paid or provided with a house), but they would want most strongly to resist the suggestion that they are not full-time.

Nevertheless it is perfectly clear to see why the suggestion is made that they are really only part-time. After all a part-time teacher is someone who works a smaller number of hours in a week than someone who is full-time. Equally a part-time doctor spends only a limited number of hours in the surgery, or wherever, compared with someone working full-time, who works correspondingly more hours. In terms of the popular use of such language it would appear that someone able to give, say, fifteen hours per week to their work as a priest or deacon in the parish is clearly not doing the same amount as someone who is spending many more hours doing the same thing. It is an argument that many stipendiary clergy will rehearse in voicing their uncertainties about non-stipendiary ministry.

Perhaps however, it is not quite so simple. There are after all the same number of hours in everyone's day. Many clergy seem somewhat obsessive about the number of hours they work and like to give the impression of incredible busy-ness. Quite whom they are seeking to impress is uncertain. My own experience of industry showed me men and women working hours and under a stress that the hardest working clergyman could never match. But even supposing that a priest claimed he was working 14 hours in a day. Of that the amount of specifically priestly work (i.e. that only he as an ordained priest is authorised to do) is small. Few priests spend all their time, or indeed much of it, engaged in sacramental acts. For the rest of their time they are engaged in studying, visiting and talking, administration (something which seems to grow and grow) and praying. The non-stipendiary priest will probably do all these things in the course of his day too, though the conversations and administration in which he will engage might well of course be far more high-powered and pressured than those of the stipendiary parish priest. Indeed if the NSM is, for example, a doctor or in an allied profession she may have many more 'important' conversations in a day than most parish priests manage in a month.

Most of what takes up a parish priest's time can be done equally well (and often is) by appropriately trained and authorised lay people. It is also true that those meetings, such as the PCC, which the parish priest will count as part of his work, the lay men and women on the same committees have to do after their 'work', but it is the same activity for both parties.

So that which is distinctly ministerial, that is to say, pertains to what only an ordained person can do, is small, and as lay ministry as a whole increasingly develops, must inevitably get smaller. The non-stipendiary priest may be doing for the majority of his day quite different things from his stipendiary colleague but each may spend exactly the same amount of the time doing those things which only they within the Christian family are actually authorised to do. And if we press the point further, it might even be argued that many people in secular employment have, by virtue of their position, many more evangelistic and counselling opportunities than their parish-based colleagues. Who would be doing the job part-time then?

I am not seeking to demean parish ministry, but it does need to be seen in perspective especially when, as does indeed happen, some stipendiary clergy are dismissive of their non-stipendiary colleagues. Of course this needs to be set within a context of the recognition that many clergy today feel under threat. Their role is increasingly unclear. Much of its former social prestige has gone and with the secularisation of society as a whole there has been a decline in the quasi-magical status sometimes accorded a priest, particularly within the catholic tradition and which gave him a sense of being 'set-apart' and special.

Many clergy feel increasingly worthless. Within the local community where once they would, as representatives of the established church, have been given pride of place, they often have to sit alongside, as one among equals, the non-conformist minister, the RC priest and even the steward of the local spiritualist church. To add insult to injury they now see men and women ordained to precisely the same ministry as themselves, able to carry on their jobs and earn considerably more than themselves. They feel that what they have regarded as so very important is now being treated as a hobby, and that hurts.

For many clergy the conflict arises over the pattern of training for the non-stipendiary ministry. Having had to spend two, three or four years in full-time training they balk at the sight of someone doing what they feel is little more than a night school or equivalent to a shortened Open

University course. Once again it is confirming their own deepest fears, that their ministry has been seriously devalued. It is in this context for example that there is often heard the jibe that the NSM is a 'back-door' to ordination.

Having seen both residential and non-residential training in operation I can only comment that both demand sacrifice, albeit often of a different kind, but that neither is obviously superior to the other. Hopefully both will be seeking to prepare men and women as fully as possible for the particular ministries to which they will be ordained, and every effort is maintained by the church authorities to ensure that standards do not differ.

The apparent loss of their particular professionalism can engender a considerable degree of pain in many stipendiary clergy which needs to be recognised. On the other hand, perhaps a wider understanding of ministry, in which there will be a number of different ministers, could free clergy to give more time to what they choose to do. In other words the new developments in ministry, of which non-stipendiary ministry is but one part, albeit of major significance, should be seen less as a problem than as an opportunity. It is not mere semantics to insist that instead of focussing upon what will be lost we need to see the potential gain.

More worrying as we consider non-stipendiary ministry as a boundary between the past and the present in the life of the Church is the capacity to force what may well indeed be a genuine new development into an existing mould. The innate conservatism of an institution such as the Church of England resists innovation until it can do no other; it then shifts its efforts into the task of modifying change so that the effects are limited. David Jenkins has said of the Church of England that it is all in favour of change provided it makes no difference! With regard to the development of non-stipendiary ministry the essential change allowing men and women to be ordained whilst continuing in their secular occupations has taken place. There is however considerable resistance to this being anything other than some kind of 'back-up' to the existing form and shape of the Church, in which NSMs can even be seen as an answer to the problem of shortage of clergy and money. Certainly if you take away the numbers of those ordained as NSMs since 1970 the numbers of those being ordained each year would fall even further behind the numbers of those retiring each year. But is this all the NSM is – merely a different style of the same thing?

From his prison cell, less than a year before he was executed for his part in the plot against Hitler, Dietrich Bonhoeffer wrote to his friend Eberhard Bethge an outline for a book. As part of the outline for one of the chapters he wrote:

> 'The church is the church only when it exists for others. To make a start, it should give away all its property to those in need. The clergy must live solely on the free-will offerings of their congregations, or possibly engage in some secular calling. The church must share in the secular problems of ordinary human life, not dominating, but helping and serving.'

It is perhaps surprising that despite all the attention that has been given to aspects of Bonhoeffer's theology the implications of his ecclesiological reflections have not been more influential. Given that clergy are representative persons, representing both the Church and its God (and whether we like it or not, in the eyes of many people both inside and outside the churches that is so) how appropriate was it that they should enjoy some kind of exalted and protected status within society? What was that saying about the Church and, more especially, the God whom they represent? Yet clergy have enjoyed privilege for hundreds of years and for hundreds of years have been manifesting an image of God and the Church which runs quite counter to the Christ whom Bonhoeffer believed was 'the man for others'. For example, when the Bishop of Ely provided the rope for the execution of starving rioters at the time of the

Littleport food riots early in the nineteenth century it was quite clear whose side he believed God was on.

Bonhoeffer looked towards an alternative future in which the representative person might be representing a wholly new image of God, one in which something of the privilege and protection of traditional clerical life would be replaced by the vulnerability of Christ as servant. Yet resistance to such an idea has been powerful. Reference has already been made to the Priest-Worker experiments that had already begun when Bonhoeffer was writing (though it is doubtful that he knew of them). It is abundantly clear that although there were considerable anxieties that priests might be 'infected' by their contact with communism, most pressing among the objections of the Roman curia to the experiment were those which feared the diminution of the protected status of those in holy orders. Among the questions put by the Holy Office to Cardinal Suhard in 1947 are the following:

> 'What is the rule of life, and what are the religious exercises, of the priests specially devoted to the service of the workers? Are there not physical, moral and religious dangers to be apprehended?
> What precautions have you in mind?'

Such anxieties have continued to be expressed, especially, though by no means exclusively, within the Roman Catholic Church. There has been, for example, considerable opposition expressed by the Pope and others to four Nicaraguan priests who served as ministers within the Sandinista government. One of them, Fernando Cardenal, a Jesuit, appointed Minister of Education in 1984, has pointed out the irony of the fact that he has now been suspended by Rome and may not function as a priest even though his present position is much more consistent with his being a priest than ever was his previous career as a professor of philosophy. He argues that it would be harder to find a more secular role for a priest than expounding Kant or

Nietzsche, whereas his present work as minister of education is actually concerned with fulfilling a gospel command to teach the uneducated.

In England of course this situation would never arise because no ordained minister of the Church of England may take a seat in the House of Commons. In another context that illustrates just how deeply ingrained within the minds of many within the churches is the link between ordination and the necessity of being kept unpolluted by the world, maintained in positions of status and power, even if the power is no more than a supposed 'spiritual' potency – the capacity to work the magic. It is precisely this however that caused such consternation to Bonhoeffer for in the figure of the ordained person, representative of Christ, there seems to be a gulf between the Church and the world, and of course ultimately between God and the world, which does serious injury to all that we believe is revealed in Christ. Even in modern services we pray 'for the church **and the world**' as if the church were not also part of the world.

To begin to see all this afresh is a major work of transformation of what has been a powerful past. Little wonder that the Church, having accepted (eventually!) the need for a non-stipendiary ministry, endeavours to domesticate it so that it merely serves to maintain the old patterns. But the NSM is standing on the boundary between the past and the present; the issues raised by standing there are not just about patterns and methods of training and preparation for ministry. In the person of the ordained minister, the representative person, major issues about how the Church understands the relationship of God and the creation are being faced. Just what sort of God do we believe in? What is God's will for a world such as ours at this time? And what sort of ministry is appropriate to communicate, proclaim and incarnate these beliefs? Those who led the Church to this boundary, Paul of Tarsus, Thomas Arnold, Roland Allen, Russell Barry and Mervyn Stockwood, to name but a few, were all people who recognised these larger questions and not merely those concerned with church order. The NSM has some kind of obligation to take their witness and their concerns seriously, and in a very real way, they are uniquely placed to do so.

CHAPTER TWO

Between Clergy and Lay

Perhaps the happiest consequence of changes in thinking about ministry that have been absorbed by the churches in recent years has been the liberation of the word 'vocation' from a certain coterie which seemed to claim it as their own. Nurses, doctors and clergymen have often experienced their particular occupations discussed in terms of hushed reverence and even if, as is no doubt often the case, speaking of their work as 'vocational' is merely a figure of speech, it is characteristic of a pattern of thought. The implicit assumption is that they have been 'called' to something higher than others and within a religious context this has sometimes been tantamount to saying that whereas some people i.e. priests, missionaries and nuns, have been called by God to something particular, the rest have to scavenge for such scraps as they can find for themselves.

In reaction to this some have wanted to speak of everyone having a vocation to their particular occupation. Although this somehow seems more fair, it doesn't do justice to reality. In the first place many people end up doing such work as they do almost by default – it was the only thing available. Then again some people go through their working lives changing jobs from time to time. Unless we extend talk of vocation to include such changes the idea breaks down, as it does if we reflect upon the fact of the large-scale unemployment of recent years. So although it may be tempting to want to speak about all people having a vocation to this or that occupation, such language causes more problems than it solves.

Quite why people do what they do is often something of a mystery. The determining factor is undoubtedly our essential disposition, which is to say, the way we are and have become by virtue of the accidents of birth and the circumstances of our growing. Some people, for example, seem to have in-built capacity for figures, others for working with wood. Some have a talent for painting, others no matter how much they study and practice are quite incapable of equalling them. We even describe some people as a 'natural', meaning that they seem to have been born with a particular talent or gift. Perhaps most people however have been born able to do many things moderately well, excelling in nothing. This is probably as well, for most of the essential jobs that enable societies to function require competence of a general and non-specific kind. Others, and apparently for no reason of their own, seem largely unable to manage even average competence in anything. Generally speaking, though inevitably not always (there are bound to be some square pegs in round holes), our dispositions and abilities will play a determining role in the sort of life we have, the jobs we get and so on.

Religious people sometimes want to describe these dispositions as God-given. For example a religious pianist might well look upon his or her abilities as a gift of God. Now, whilst I am not wanting to denigrate the sincerity of such a belief, nor to say that Christians will not want to use such capacities as they have to the glory of God and the service of mankind, nevertheless we need to exercise considerable caution in our use of such language. For whilst many would want to see musical talent of an unusual kind as something for which to be profoundly grateful, the implications of the belief that it is 'God-given' are profound.

Is it to mean that everything we are and have, and, by inference therefore, all that we are not and do not have, are equally God-given? Does it mean that human inabilities and disabilities are equally God-given? That would be a serious claim, for it would presumably mean that physical and mental handicaps would also have to be looked upon as God-given, or inflicted, as perhaps it would be more appropriate to describe them. If we balk at that idea, and I suggest we should (the consequences of the alternative being morally unacceptable) then we need to re-assess the claims that positive abilities are a divine gift because it may help us understand more clearly just what we mean by vocation.

It is not that I am wanting to debunk the idea of vocation so much as to find ways in which we can speak about it in terms which do not thereby demean those who do not feel a sense of call of any kind. In practice I would suggest this means we come to recognise that it is not God who calls people to become ministers but the Church, and that ordination be seen as the consecration of what the Church presents before God. One knows just too much about the political jockeying that makes up ecclesiastical life to imagine that God chooses diocesan bishops (though some will press the unprovable point that it is precisely through such machinations that God acts; frankly I just do not believe it). No less is this so in the case of the lower clergy. The Church, hopefully under the guidance of God, tests and examines those offering themselves, and then has to decide and be responsible for the decision made.

In practice the Church does not in fact make much use of the idea of 'calling' in its selection procedures. It is true that in the ordination service there is a question asked of the candidates about their sense of calling, but in the processes of selection a sense of having been called will not normally score high on the list of things for which selectors are looking. Perhaps we have all been somewhat misled by accounts of unusual conversion experiences such as that of St Paul. By very far the majority of those who offer themselves for ordination do not advance such an experience as the foundation of their coming forward, and selectors would, on the whole, not allow themselves to be swayed by the claims of candidates that God had told them quite clearly that they were to be ordained.

Conversion experiences do happen of course, though usually (and wasn't this as much the case with Paul?) as the end result of a, sometimes unconscious, process. Just because someone lays claim to an experience does not mean the Church is obliged to accept it at face value, and, as with Paul, there has to be a clear examination of someone in terms of all that they are and whether it accords with the job that is going, before they can be accepted.

The circumstances whereby men and women feel that from somewhere within them has arisen a sense that they might like to think about the possibility of ordination vary enormously from person to person. Though it is tempting for some to imagine that a strong sense of 'call' ought to be regarded more highly than the tentative searching of another person, the Church is quite right not to see matters in such black and white terms. After all God works through our dispositions and because they vary so much it is inevitable that the ways in which we respond to God through them will differ enormously. There is no right and wrong way.

For many people who consider non-stipendiary ministry the 'cause' of their first thinking about this as a possibility may well be the deepening sense of life-change that comes about in middle age. A Roman Catholic priest, an Anglican vicar and a Rabbi were once asked when they thought life began. The Catholic priest at once replied that it began at the moment of conception. The Anglican responded that he felt it began when the foetus was about six weeks old when the first tissues of the central nervous system appeared. The rabbi thought for a while and then said he thought life began when the mortgage was paid off and the kids had left home! Certainly for many people such an age is one of enormous crisis, when perhaps the most important questions have to be faced about oneself and the rest of life. Dante's *Divine Comedy* begins 'Midway in the course of our life', and many therapists and analysts recognise that what is sometimes called the 'mid-life crisis' is potentially the time of real opportunity.

Because candidates for non-stipendiary ministry have

to be over thirty years of age, it is not unusual for many 'vocations' to have originated in precisely this milieu, and there is no doubt that those who have begun to face up to these crises of middle age have, because they have been able to face up to the possibilities of change, a great deal to offer others through their ministry.

For some the possibility of ordination resolves for them issues and questions which perhaps originated a good number of years earlier but which had been neglected or deliberately ignored. The pressures of early life do not always lend themselves to the sort of commitment demanded by ordination, and for many people there has perhaps been the inner urge to explore something more of oneself and the world before making some kind of final commitment. There are people too who have only just heard about non-stipendiary ministry and whilst some years ago they had given some thought to the idea of ordination, they felt unable to make a commitment to stipendiary ministry because other sides of their nature required proper expression in their work, or in the need to have children or whatever.

For many people the origin of the idea of offering for ordination comes from others, perhaps the parish priest or another member of the local church, who has seen and recognised the potential of a particular person, usually on the basis of their 'track record' within the life of the local church. In those churches where leadership is already shared and ministries of various kinds regarded as the norm, such a person will already have shown their ability to exercise a style of ministry which naturally exhibits the sort of qualities needed in an ordained minister. Certainly anyone who wants to be accepted as a candidate for the non-stipendiary ministry will need to be in good standing in the life of her or his local church, someone who has already shown that they have the potential for what is demanded by the ordained ministry.

Before any candidate can be considered there are certain

things which need to be clear. The first is an indication from the PCC that they are willing to accept and support this candidate in the particular ministry for which they would be ordained. The incumbent has to present a confidential report to selectors and it is clear that only in exceptional circumstances would someone be accepted if this report was essentially unfavourable. And it is right that this is so, for the ordained ministry does not exist to serve the religious needs of an individual who is seeking some kind of religious fulfilment thereby, but to enable the Church to forward the kingdom of God through the particular manifestation of that authority given to the minister in ordination in the life of the Church, locally and universally. Those in secular work also need to obtain a reference from their employer.

An official ACCM report describes the Selectors' task as follows:

> . . . to estimate the strength and genuineness of a candidate's vocation, to identify their particular call and to test it against their proposed form of ministry, and to assess their ability to work out this vocation in the years which lie ahead. The call to Christian commitment as a lay person must not be confused with the call to professional ministries. Does the sense of ministry arise primarily from a neurotic need? It is particularly important to judge the ways in which the call has already influenced the life and work of the candidate. Has it strengthened their devotional life? Has it already shown itself in pastoral awareness? Has it persisted long enough to ensure that it will last? Has the candidate really thought out the implications of a life-time of service? Have they made a real contribution to the life of their parish church or college chapel? Have they thought through the message of the gospel and their contribution to spreading it?
>
> In making these assessments of the candidate's vocation it is necessary to bear in mind that apart from what might be regarded as public activities − taking services, preaching, chairing committees etc. − the minister will be largely needed in the more private activities of dealing with people in a pastoral way and acting as reconciler, healer and enabler.

> (ACCM Paper 12, 1983 − *inclusive language changes my own*)

Bishops' regulations for the non-stipendiary ministry are quite clear that candidates are to be assessed on the basis of exactly the same criteria as those for the stipendiary ministry. Equally the standards for training are the same. This is of course exactly how it should be. Every priest or deacon, however they earn their money, is a priest or deacon solely by virtue of their ordination. There are not first and second-class priests, neither is there some kind of First XV contrasted with the replacements or substitutes in case the 'real' team are injured. A deacon is a deacon and a priest is a priest.

Ordination is not a matter of personal fulfilment; no one is ordained priest or deacon purely to satisfy their inward needs or wishes. It is an ordination *by* the Church *for* the Church, and the only meaning the diaconate and priesthood has lies in this recognition. In practical terms this means ordination to the life of a local community, or in the case of a bishop to a diocese, for he is there to be an overseer of the local communities in his area. So-called 'diocesan officials' if they are in the order of priest or deacon ought (theologically at least, though it is an area in which the Church of England has long been unclear) to be members of a local church and in which they exercise those ministries for which they have been ordained. Particular gifts are given for particular tasks, and those pertaining to the ministries of deacon and priest are in essence concerned with the life of the local eucharistic community.

Every NSM is therefore part of the life of some parish and the particular ministry to which she or he has been ordained is primarily exercised within the life of that eucharistic community, though of course may also be exercised, on occasion, elsewhere within the church. Ordination, at least in the Church of England, is ordination in the Church of God, and not something merely limited to the boundaries of a particular congregation. This is not to suggest that there is not and cannot be such a thing as a 'work-based' ministry, something which many NSMs are concerned to promote (and which will figure prominently in the following chapter), but simply to indicate a point of fact and logic, that the diaconate and priesthood are ministries whose *raison d'être* is to be found within the life of a community. So whilst it may well be important to recognise that the work situations of particular men and women may present them with particular opportunities in the exercise of their ministry, nevertheless it is fundamental to the meaning of ordination as deacon or priest, as the Church of England has understood it, that all those thus ordained exercise these ministries within local eucharistic communities, in the life of the local church.

This point is strengthened by the pattern of training for the NSM. Whereas most clergy have been prepared for ordination by means of residential training (though by no means all; increasing numbers are preparing for stipendiary ministry on non-residential courses), the majority of NSMs prepare non-residentially. This means that by far the greater amount of their practical preparation happens in their home church where the incumbent is a major partner in the process of ministerial formation. Not only does he assist in the training process but he often will take part in the assessment procedure. In this he is of course helped by the members of the local church who will constantly be feeding back to him, in various ways, their own responses to the new 'student'. There is much to be gained by this process. It means for example that it ought to be relatively impossible for the student to switch personae, to put on the face of a cleric. The local church should be able to see through that and help prevent it.

This is seen as one possible way in which the NSM can assist in the de-clericalisation of the church, of breaking down the alleged distinction between clergy and lay. For whilst she or he is most definitely a 'real' ordained minister, at the same time she or he is more like the ordinary 'lay' members of the Church in terms of lifestyle. This can of course be a major obstruction to their being accepted. Both clergy and lay alike can often wish to perpetuate a role observance which makes life easier for both. The priest who maintains a distinctive, 'set apart', role may well find considerable security thereby. His parishioners too might like to collude with him in this, for it enables them to project all sorts of fantasies on to him whereby they are enabled to escape from their own obligations. They can then see themselves as essentially a support group for the vicar, a much easier role than seeing themselves as the chief agents of the kingdom of God for which task the vicar exists to serve and support them.

This serves to focus attention upon what is understood by the 'set-apartness' of the ordained ministry. It is a powerful tradition going back to the earliest days of the Church. St Ignatius of Antioch, writing early in the second century, could be said to be the first writer to describe the ordained ministry in exalted terms:

> 'Your obedience to your bishop, as though he were Christ Jesus, shows me plainly enough that yours is no worldly manner of life, but that of Jesus Christ himself, who gave his life for us that faith in his death might save you from death. At the same time, however, essential as it is that you should never act independently of the bishop – as evidently you do not – you must also be submissive to your clergy, and regard them as apostles of Jesus Christ our hope in whom we shall one day be found, if our lives are lived in him. The deacons too, who serve the mysteries of Jesus Christ, must be men universally approved in every way . . .
>
> Equally, it is for the rest of you to hold the deacons in as great respect as Jesus Christ; just as you should look on the bishops as a type of the Father, and the clergy as the apostolic circle forming his council; for without these three orders no church has any right to the name.'

('To the Trallians')

Such sentiments were increasingly echoed in later years, and especially after the conversion of Constantine. Thus it was that St John Chrysostom could write of the priesthood:

'What priests do on earth God ratifies above . . . Indeed he has given them nothing less than the whole authority of heaven. For he says "Whose soever sins ye forgive, they are forgiven, and whose soever ye retain they are retained". What authority could be greater than that? "The Father hath given all judgment unto the Son". But I see that the Son has placed it all in their hands.'

(On the Priesthood)

and again:

'Do you not know what the priest is? He is an angel of the Lord. And they his own words that he speaks? If you despise him, you do not despise him, but God who ordained him . . . If God does not work through him, then there is no baptism, nor communion in the mysteries, nor blessing; you are no longer Christians.'

(2nd Homily on Timothy 2–3)

Understandable though it is that such language came to be employed, it is nevertheless hard to equate it with the injunctions of Jesus about service as the essence of his own ministry and to which he was committing his disciples. Perhaps the change occurred during the later part of the first century when earlier models of ministry were being traded for later, some of which bore upon them the stamp of extraneous material. Certainly at first in the life of the Church, as it is reflected in the New Testament, there was considerable variation in the practice of ministry. It is clear, for example, that the pattern within the Church in Jerusalem in the years immediately after the Resurrection, firmly centred upon Peter, changed in the second decade. Jesus' brother James begins to emerge as a leader of a strongly Jewish sect, even though he had no credentials as an apostle in the sense in which this was originally conceived (i.e. as having been appointed by Jesus as one of the twelve). It has been suggested by some historians that the first idea of a 'set-apart' ministry originated with James, whom, it is alleged, claimed for himself rights of leadership based upon the same principles of heredity that characterised the office of High Priest in the old covenant.

Simultaneously, as the Church spread outwards, different patterns of ministry were emerging. In Antioch for example the pattern seems to have been centred upon what the Acts of the Apostles calls 'prophets and teachers' (13.1–3). Lists in the first letter to the Corinthians (1 Cor. 12.28) and that to the Ephesians (4.11–13) point to an even greater diversity, a situation confirmed and reflected in the Pastoral epistles (e.g. 1 Tim. 3.1–13; 4.14; 5.17–22; Titus 1.5–9). Although institutions always tend towards further institutionalisation, such that the eventual standardization was inevitable, the patterns that emerge still reflect a view of ministry which was essentially functional.

The change towards a view of ordination as being more than functional, (sometimes called 'ontological', which is to say a view that the ordained ministers were 'set apart' not merely to perform different tasks but were receiving thereby some kind of permanent 'character' on their very selves or souls) can, in part at least, be attributed to the influence of the Roman understanding of 'ordination'. The Latin verb *ordinare* refers to the practice of appointing to office and setting in order. Within the life of Rome there was a special élite known as the *ordo clarissimus*, the Roman Senate, which brought with it not merely responsibility but also considerable privilege and prestige. An *ordo* was a particular row or line separating different levels of honour. Once such an idea had been incorporated into the thinking of the Church, and after the conversion of Constantine this was to be normative, it is not difficult to see how prestige and distinction adhered to the role of deacon, priest and bishop.

This understanding seems significantly far removed from the patterns of the New Testament. Use of the verb *ordinare* in the Latin translation has altogether different connotations from the Greek word *cheironteo*, which is also used to describe someone elected or appointed to office by show of hands (e.g. Acts 14.23 and 2 Cor. 8.19). This is linked to the laying on of hands (*epethēkan athtois tas cheiras*) described in e.g. Acts 6.6; 13.3; 19.6; 1 Tim 4.14; and 2 Tim 1.6. That translation and its effect on the Church in Rome has had major consequences for the whole Church in subsequent centuries.

Perhaps however the greatest damage done by such an understanding has been to the teaching of Jesus, something which the Statement on Ministry by the World Council of Churches (in the so-called LIMA Report of *Baptism, Eucharist, Ministry*) is at pains to emphasise:

> 'The authority of the ordained ministry is not to be understood as the possession of the ordained person but as a gift for the continuing edification of the body in and for which the minister has been ordained. Authority has the character of responsibility before God and is exercised with the co-operation of the whole community.
>
> Christ's authority ... is confirmed by his life of service, and, supremely, by his death and resurrection. Authority in the Church can only be authentic as it seeks to conform to this model.'

(Sections 15 and 16)

Dom Gregory Dix, in a famous purple passage in his great work on the Eucharist *The Shape of the Liturgy* comments on the instruction of Jesus to 'do this in remembrance of me': 'Was ever a command so obeyed?'. It would be difficult to feel likewise about Jesus' words on the subject of ministry:

> 'You know that, among the Gentiles, rulers lord it over their subjects, and the great make their authority felt. It shall not be so with you; among you, whoever wants to be great must be your servant, and whoever wants to be first must be the slave of all – just as the Son of Man did not come to be served but to serve, and to give his life as a ransom for many.'

(Matthew 20.25ff)

Far too much thinking about ministry has been concerned with the minutiae of the performance of the office, and far too little with the end for which it exists. It is certainly worth noting that the Lima statement begins with the needs which the Church exists to serve and only then proceeds to speak about the ordained ministry in relation to them:

> 'The churches need to work from the perspective of the calling of the whole people of God. A common answer needs to be found to the following questions: How, according to the will of God and under the guidance of the Holy Spirit, is the life of the Church to be understood and ordered, so that the Gospel may be spread and the community built up in love?
>
> 'As heralds and ambassadors, ordained ministers are representatives of Jesus Christ to the community, and proclaim his message of reconciliation. As leaders and teachers they call the community to submit to the authority of Jesus Christ . . As pastors, under Jesus Christ the chief shephered, they assemble and guide the dispersed people of God.'

(Sections 6, 11)

Because the NSM is clearly not 'set apart' from others in the obvious sense that other clergy have sometimes seemed to be or have wished to give the impression of (their clothing is the most obvious example of this), it is to be hoped that their presence within the life of the local church can help the people of God as a whole begin again to focus aright their attention away from the particular office-holder and towards the work for which they have been ordained. Investing clergy with a quasi-magical status is not only bad for the clergy, and bad for the laity, it is also bad theology.

Yet it is not merely a very high doctrine of priesthood which has served to isolate the clergy. Whether we like it or not, status and class have unquestionably played a major part in the thinking of many people about the clergy, at least in so far as the Church of England is concerned. Even though the traditional image of the clergyman as being the product of a public school and an ancient university is gradually breaking down (though quite slowly, especially at the episcopal level), nevertheless the manner of life of many stipendiary clergy still elevates them to a level at which it remains difficult for many lay people to relate to them properly, and which, in turn, serves to hinder their capacity to minister effectively.

In many, especially inner-city, parishes, the Vicarage will often be, by a long way, the best house. We once lived on a council estate in inner-city Leeds, and even there, where we too were in a local authority house, somehow or other it managed to be the biggest and best. Wherever it is situated, it will usually be surrounded by a garden and afforded a measure of privacy which at once places it in a position superior to that experienced by many parishioners. In my experience many clergy just do not grasp just how much courage is required to bring someone to the Vicarage door, even if only to make an enquiry about baptism. The parsonage house remains a significant mental barrier.

There is also about the lifestyle of clergy a freedom which once again isolates them from the experience of the majority of those among whom they minister. That freedom is of course something to be cherished and although a stipend is not huge (though neither is it so bad, especially when taken with the house and other perks, including, these days, the payment of the Poll Tax for the ordained minister and spouse), it is intended to free the minister to use the time for her work without other constraints. Once again however this freedom isolates clergy from the experience of others. They are unlikely to be made redundant and although some dioceses have introduced voluntary systems of pastoral care for clergy, they are (especially those enjoying a free-hold) under no obligation to give any sort of account of themselves to anyone.

The response of some clergy to this, a response largely motivated by guilt, is to make frantic efforts to convince everyone they meet how busy they are, and indeed sometimes they seem to engage in frenetic activity to justify their words. The reality is of course that they thereby prove the point of just how unlike others they are.

The ordained minister in secular employment rarely enjoys a similar liberty. Their working hours will be severely constrained by the demands of others and the confines of the particular institutions and organisations for which they work. Like the majority of lay members of the Church they have to fit Church-related activities – PCCs, Study Groups and so on, into their spare time after work, quite often when their very best has been demanded by and given to a secular employer. Unlike parochial clergy they do not enjoy the possibility of taking time off at some other time in the day prior to an evening meeting, and indeed that which a parish priest regards as part of his official work, i.e. that for which he is paid, the NSM and other 'working' people do voluntarily. Perhaps even more important than time boundaries, what differentiates NSMs from their stipendiary colleagues are the degrees of accountability which increasingly characterise secular employment, and, with them, pressures related to performance which parochial clergy just cannot appreciate. Even working in a theological college, which is hardly the cut-and-thrust world of industry and high finance, I am subject to an appraisal and constrained by performance-related time boundaries wholly unknown to me within parish life.

This is not to say that parish clergy do not inhabit the 'real' world nor to poke fun at them for something for which they are largely not responsible, it is simply to be clear about the different sort of lifestyle which characterises ministry when exercised by a stipendiary and a non-stipendiary person. It is also to advance the argument by recognising that although stipendiary ministry gives a particular freedom to the minister to be used by him or her, so equally the constraints which characterise the secular employment of the NSM can be seen as a particular opportunity in the fulfilment of their own ministry.

This can be illustrated by reference to two aspects of

teaching and preaching in relation to spirituality and the Christian's secular involvement. In terms of spirituality for example, the stipendiary minister can organise his or her time around the need for space and time to pray. If they choose they can give themselves an hour or more each morning and organise their whole day to make this possible. In addition they can provide a set of weekday services which minister to their own needs as much as those of others. Within that time for prayer there will often be space to say a full office, consisting of psalms and readings, time for intercession etc. It will often also be possible to find space for silent meditation or to experiment with prayer. In addition, many clergy will try and find a week when they can get right away from it all in a retreat house, and in many dioceses parishes are encouraged to provide financial support for this. All of which is made possible by the absence of constraints upon stipendiary clergy (and clearly it is something to be encouraged). The problems begin when the sort of pattern the clergy take for granted, itself a kind of diluted monasticism, is then used by them as the principal model offered to others.

Some of those whose lives offer them a fair amount of spare time may well, of course, discover such a pattern to be a well from which they can themselves draw. I have, for example, sometimes discovered housebound people who have believed themselves called to a ministry of intercession. Equally I have known single and divorced men and women who have sought to use their freedom from marital ties in order to devote themselves to prayer and theological study. For these people the experience of the clergy as they seek to make space and time for the life of prayer will be invaluable.

Unfortunately such people are rare, and for the majority the sort of lifestyle which allows the clergy to make the choices they do (whatever they do with them) is something which lies quite outside their own experience. Many people live wholly at the mercy of the decisions of others. At work for example they are bound to fulfil the demands of an employer or an organisation in which from time to time, they will inhabit a moral world which is extremely murky. The time boundaries of their work will be tightly defined, which taken together with the demands of a family and the need for recreation and sleep will place severe limitations upon the amount of time which might possibly be called 'free'. In addition to this many people just do not have space for privacy in their homes and certainly there is often an absence of anything approaching silence. In such a context the idea that people say an office, or find time each morning for a short period of silent prayer or reading is simply unrealistic, and when clergy go on suggesting such things the end result is often a considerable degree of guilt in those who have no reason for it.

The NSM in secular employment is at the mercy of the same pressures as other Christians in secular employment. She too has to arrive at the office, the factory or the school at a certain time or face the consequences. She too has a family to get moving in the morning before she can herself get off to work, and then in the evening there is food to be prepared, family to be received and listened to. There may also be work brought home. Teachers have a great deal to do in the evening but so do the vast majority of men and women in industry, and even when there is not, there is more often than not a great deal of tiredness which comes from the pressures of the day.

For an NSM to find time to pray is not easy. Some NSMs in training discover early on how difficult it is to fit in their studies in the midst of a busy life and once they are ordained these pressures do not diminish. Many of course do not have a study or a room they can call their own (one NSM did his three years of study on a table in the hall!), so the actual mechanics of prayer are difficult even before beginning – but then what? The idea that men and women in secular employment can find time to say Mattins and Evensong each day (as Canon Law specifies) is a nonsense. Of course some may be able to do so, but most will not.

Perhaps one of the most important things which the NSM has to offer lay men and women in the life of the local church is their struggle to find patterns of spirituality appropriate to life today. If they can, then they will indeed have discovered a great treasure, but the awesome nature of the task should not be underestimated.

On the course for which I work, we have a member of staff whose major responsibility is for spiritual formation, and the college with which we are linked also enjoys the presence of a tutor in spirituality on whom we can draw. This means that we are able to approach this issue with sufficient time and attention, convinced that their whole formation for ministry depends closely on being able to encourage those men and women who are preparing with us to discover for themselves a sustainable pattern of life that can feed and nourish them in years to come. Because many of our students work in contexts which do not always lend themselves to a simple and straightforward morality, where white is white and black is black, it is also vital that praying is real enough to recognise the nature of compromise as making enormous spiritual demands. We would not pretend that as yet we have produced answers to all the questions but we do think there are grounds for believing that we are making significant strides, as students and staff together, towards such a spirituality. It is also good to be sharing in this process with others who are making their own distinctive contributions to the search. A number of recent books too, such as Gerry Hughes' *God of Surprises* and Kathleen Fischer's *Women at the Well* are proving themselves enormously helpful in this task of appropriate spiritual formation.

The foundation of the pattern with which we are working lies above all in honesty and thus can only flow out of the particular circumstances of our life — who we are and why, where we are, and not merely what we want to be, itself sometimes little more than an exercise in fantasy and escapism. In the belief that God encounters is in what is, and not in what is not, our spirituality, our response to God must therefore be rooted in the reality of our daily existence. It needs to be related to our family circumstances, to our developing understanding of who we are as persons in relationship with others, to the demands made upon us in our workplace or perhaps in the reality of being unemployed, or employed in the context of a home and community. It requires too a sensitivity to issues of justice and the whole realm of the political. Above all it needs to flow out of the reality of God's being in all of this and our struggle to discover and discern that presence. For that reason such a pattern of spirituality will be deeply biblical, in the sense of recognising a God who encounters us within history (and not merely in some kind of unearthly 'spiritual' realm), but in no way biblicist, in the sense of our imagining that any past experience of God can be wholly determinative of the creative possibilities of the future. As Peter Selby has written:

> '. . . theology by recalling and interpreting the New Testament resurrection proclamation maintains man's openness to the possibility that the God who raised Jesus from the dead will perform the radically new in our time.'
>
> (Selby 1976, p. 163)

At the present time there is much dissatisfaction within the Church about the Daily Office (and in particular with the wholly unimaginative and outstandingly dull form of it offered within the ASB). Cranmer's masterpiece of Mattins and Evensong was a genuine leap forward from the monastic offices of the later medieval period. Beautiful though it can still be, the BCP largely provides little more than an irrelevant counterpoint to the pressures and complexities with which many people have now to live. Some still want such an escape route, but for those who believe that God has to be responded to within these pressures and complexities something quite different is required.

I do not believe the stipendiary parish clergy can provide

this, nor are the suggestions of Fr George Guiver particularly helpful (in an otherwise first class book on the development of the daily office – *The Company of Voices*), that the Daily Prayer of the Church be carried out in the parish churches by the stipendiary clergy and others and to which those unable to be present, as it were, 'tune in' as and when they can. The model not only remains too clerical and quasi-monastic (though that is not wholly surprising for after all he is a monk), it just does not help people see prayer as the means of engaging more seriously with the realities of the world because that is where God is to be encountered and responded to.

Perhaps the best 'form' of daily prayer which I have encountered, and begun to draw students' attention to, is that used by the Little Gidding Community of Christ the Sower, which does at least have the virtue of providing a solid biblical foundation to undergird an active life of work but which does not require time which is simply unavailable. It also provides for the possibility of gatherings, say once a week, of people engaged in secular employment for sharing and communicating and celebrating a simple eucharist. In subsequent years more and more experimenting will be required, and in this the NSM has a most important part to play, for the patterns of spirituality which the Church needs as it enters the last decade of the century must belong genuinely to the whole 'laos', the whole people of God and their concerns. The NSM, inhabiting their world, and with her training, is exactly positioned to do such pioneering.

The second way in which the NSM can be of particular use to the laity in their discipleship is through their whole approach to their work and other secular involvement. As this is the main substance of the following chapter the only thing that need be said here is that the NSM can legitimately be seen as a role-model for other Christians in their work. In the ordination service, candidates are asked by the Bishop:

'Will you strive to fashion your own life and that of your household according to the way of Christ?'

In their affirmative reply the candidate is acknowledging that clergy are public figures and correspondingly need to be serious about what that means. It does not mean they are expected to behave differently from other Christians but a recognition that they are someone to whom other Christians will look. In part this is their representative role within the life of the Church. In consequence, if they then behave in a way which suggests that the Church and its concerns must take precedence over, what many Christians still call, 'the world' and its concerns, they are role-modelling an understanding of God and his concerns which I believe to be wholly inadequate. For example, if there is a clash between a meeting of the PCC or the Bible Study Group and a branch meeting of the NSM's trade union, the option made provides other Christian members with a clear indication of where they should be applying their own energies. In my own experience, this particular choice is not one easily understood by stipendiary parish-based clergy, and unquestionably it may cause uncomfortable questions to be asked, but the NSM cannot evade such complexity, even if the incumbent cannot see anything that matters more to God's kingdom than the PCC!

In such things the NSM offers to the laity of the Church something vital to their own discipleship. A pattern of praying that does justice to the complexities of their existence, and a pattern of appropriate involvement in the reality of work, is often precisely that for which many lay Christians look to their clergy and are usually denied. This is not the fault of stipendiary clergy, it is simply a consequence of the way the Church has been and, in many places still is. Of course, simply having an NSM on the staff of a parish does not automatically mean that such things will now be sorted out. Much will depend on the NSM in question and it cannot be denied that some are more churchy than a clutch of clergy, but if such things have begun to be faced in the course of preparation for ministry then at least there can be a legitimate hope that ordination will not have the effect of putting an end to the process of searching and struggling.

Seeing the NSM as a role-model in this way raises questions about the precise relationship between those ministries which are being exercised by lay people and that which is distinctive to the ordained minister. If the NSM is on the boundary between clergy and ordained, where exactly is the boundary drawn? What is the difference between an ordained minister and a lay person?

Some NSM training courses (such as that for which I work) may have a tendency to draw too sharp a line of demarcation between ordained and lay simply by virtue of isolating those in training and preparing them for ordination in a way that emphasises tasks and a role which pertain only to the ordained minister *qua* ordained minister. Some other courses (sometimes for financial rather than ideological reasons) whilst helping to maintain a strong sense of the boundary by doing ministerial formation alongside lay training, are in danger of not making the distinction clear enough.

Ordination as a deacon or priest is at one level simply an authorisation to perform particular and distinctive tasks within the life of the people of God, and thus different only in terms of function from other, 'lay', ministries (which may include quasi-ministerial tasks such as preaching, conducting certain services, taking funerals, preparing for baptism and marriage etc.). At another level however it is something quite distinctive. Section 13 of the Lima document states:

> The chief responsibility of the ordained ministry is to assemble and build up the body of Christ by proclaiming and teaching the Word of God, by celebrating the sacraments, and by guiding the life of the community in its worship, its mission and its caring ministry.

The central understanding this offers of the role of the ordained ministry is that of leadership and teaching, and the

Lima statement clearly sees these particular functions as indissolubly linked to the idea of permanence:

> In order to fulfil its mission, the Church needs persons who are publicly and continually responsible for pointing to its fundamental dependence on Jesus Christ, and thereby provide, within a multiplicity of gifts, a focus of its unity.
>
> (Section 8)

Here the ordained ministry is clearly recognised as having a visible, representative role. In terms of the Church relating to those outside its membership this role needs to be both recognisable and permanent. For this reason ordination is regarded as being 'for life' and not merely a temporary office. In terms too of its representative role within the Church the permanence manifests the permanence of God's covenant with his people.

Thus the ordained ministers of the Church are different from those exercising lay ministries in terms of the particular commissioning they receive. The Lima document speaks of ordination in three phases:

> '. . . an invocation that the new minister be given the power of the Holy Spirit in the new relation which is established between this minister and the local Christian community and, by intention, the Church universal.
>
> . . . a sign of the granting of this prayer by the Lord . . . in confidence that God, being faithful to his promise in Christ, enters sacramentally into contingent, historical forms of human relationship and uses them for his purpose.
>
> . . . an acknowledgement by the Church of the gifts of the Spirit in the one ordained.
>
> (Sections 42–44)

In those churches in which the ordained minister has traditionally been visibly 'set apart', the ordination of a new, non-stipendiary, minister can be a new visible sign to the whole people of God of their own call to ministry. In those where some kind of 'every member ministry' is normative, it will be important to recognise that the newly-

ordained minister takes her or his place among other minis-
ters but that to this particular ministry has been given, by
the wider church, distinctive and life-long responsibilities.
This is perfectly expressed in what the Lima report calls
'Guiding Principles for the Exercise of the Ordained
Ministry':

> 'It should be **personal**, because the presence of Christ among
> his people can most effectively be pointed to by the person
> ordained to proclaim the Gospel and to call the community
> to serve the Lord in unity of life and witness. It should also be
> **collegial**, for there is a need of for a college or ordained
> ministers sharing in the common task of representing the
> concerns of the community. Finally, the intimate relationship
> between the ordained ministry and the community should
> find expression in a **communal** dimension where the exercise
> of the ordained ministry is rooted in the life of the community
> and requires the community's effective participation in the
> discovery of God's will and the guidance of the Spirit.
>
> (Section 32)

A ministry which is personal, collegiate and communal,
ought to be avoiding some of the pitfalls referred to above in
terms of ordination being a doorway to the exercise and
abuse of power. In this respect the non-stipendiary ministry
can help to bridge the gap between the clergy and the laity,
between the so-called 'professional' Christian and the
amateurs.

Most of the emphasis so far in this chapter has been on the
opportunities presented by non-stipendiary ministry for the
development of the laity at the level of the life of the local
church. It does however also have important consequences
for diocesan structures for one of the issues being thrown up
by the experience of many NSMs is the realisation of just
how much the structures of diocesan and deanery life are
clerically orientated.

The clergy are grouped in deaneries, usually geographi-
cally based, and the structures of communication within the
life of the Church are based upon a pyramidal model

whereby information is fed downwards from bishops to rural deans, and from rural deans to the parish clergy at their chapter meetings. Such information as PCCs receive about the diocese and wider church tends to come through this, often well-filtered, channel. There is of course meant to be a parallel channel which incorporates the laity, by means of diocesan and deanery synods, but in practice the former pattern predominates. There is, I suppose, an inevitability about this. In an organisation, such as the Church, made up of both paid and voluntary workers, management structures will naturally have a greater degree of purchase on the lives of those who are actually dependent upon them than those who are not.

Clergy chapters tend to meet monthly, mostly during the day-time, and many of them incorporate worship, study and a meal (often breakfast). NSMs are full members of their deanery chapter but in many cases, because of the timing of the meeting, it is just not possible for them to attend. Some chapters endeavour to accomodate their NSMs by arranging one or two evening meetings in the course of a year, but most parish clergy do not like such meetings, and very few chapters are willing to meet on a Saturday (when, in any case, the NSM in secular employment ought to be having the chance of a rest with the family). In consequence most NSMs discover that not only are they denied access to important areas of ministerial life, but more especially to an important structure of Church life. It is a testimony to the fact that in practice many NSMs feel that their stipendiary colleagues regard them as 'second class', but more especially that the structures of ecclesiastical life exist primarily to serve a narrowly-conceived clerical machine.

If the Church is to begin to take NSM seriously it means not only having to re-think just what it means and understands by ministry but also recognising that the structures which support and maintain it have to change. Some dioceses have attempted to circumvent the problem by drafting

NSMs into a chapter of their own. Although this gives the appearance of taking NSM seriously it does not actually deal with the real problem, which is to say, the management structures upon which much most of the life of the Church is built.

Those structures are closely linked with status. The ascending order of ecclesiastical titles – plain Reverend, Canon, Rural Dean (an inner-city anachronism if ever there was one!), Venerable, Very Reverend, Right Reverend, Most Reverend – makes a nonsense of a community whose Lord warned against those who liked to be greeted respectfully with grand titles (Matthew 23.7–12).

An NSM of my acquaintance is employed by a major corporation as a management and communication consultant. His highly skilled job is to make sure there is effective communication within the company. After ordination he attended his first Diocesan Synod and was appalled to discover how badly it was run. He wrote to his diocesan bishop offering his services and skills with a view to facilitating future meetings. The bishop thanked him politely but refused his offer on the grounds that the organisation of the diocesan synod was something that needed to be done by an archdeacon. Presumably status is to be preferred to effective functioning!

NSMs are, mercifully, freed from the concerns of many clergy with regard to preferment and status. On the other hand, as members of the human race and working in secular organisations, they recognise the issues that are involved in such concerns, and indeed they will no doubt have a major investment in the processes of furthering their own career. Their presence within the structures of the Church, albeit at such levels a marginal presence, has highlighted the extent to which such issues matter to clergy but are largely unacknowledged. Coming from secular organisations which have learned how essential to successful functioning proper systems of support and appraisal are, they are often appalled at how ineffective the structures of Church life are, and in particular, at how little support is offered to the clergy. Unquestionably a good number of clergy would be extremely hesitant before accepting the need for management consultants to assist them in their planning, and others would balk at the prospect of mandatory appraisal, but this is largely because they have yet to grasp that such things are done not to find fault but to improve not only the quality of the work but also to provide greater support for their work.

Because the NSM has less investment in the career structure of clerical life than her stipendiary colleagues she is ideally placed to promote a more open discussion about what is often a covert issue. Like them of course she will be 'on file' at the Bishop's office, a file to which she has no right of access. A recent move to include one section in which ministers have the right to give an account of themselves, and which they may request the right to amend at any time, has merely served to heighten rather than diminish anxiety about these files because it has drawn attention to the fact that the other contents of the file, which include official observations on the minister and which may have considerable influence on future employers, remain secret. It is an intolerable situation in what is meant to be a community built on trust and love.

The boundary between the clergy and the laity has been important throughout the past history of the Church and to this day it remains highly influential in terms of the mechanics of ecclesiastical life. Major issues such as the question of the ordination of women to the priesthood or the question of uniting with the Methodists have in effect been decided by the House of Clergy in General Synod exercising a veto. The theological rationale for the maintenance of a separate House of Clergy is unclear and although a case could be made for having clergy to represent clergy in the processes of synod, it seems wholly unjustified to have such a disproportionate number of them exercising such a powerful hold upon the rest of the Church. If we really are the whole people of God (*laos*, meaning people, includes the clergy too) then the whole idea of ordination being about membership of some exclusive sect needs a major examination.

Simply ordaining more and more non-stipendiary ministers will not of course simply transform the structures of Church life overnight. Nevertheless it is clear that the presence of NSMs is bringing to the fore a number of key issues, both theological and practical, about the relationship of the clergy to the whole people of God. To have men and women standing where the NSM does, between the two, at a time when, because of falling numbers of stipendiary clergy, more and more NSMs are being drawn into stipendiary ministry, may well prove increasingly difficult, but for the sake of the Church it is to be hoped that they will continue to do so.

CHAPTER THREE

Between the Church and the Kingdom of God

Perhaps one of the most confusing and misunderstood aspects of non-stipendiary ministry is to be found in the idea of a 'ministry in the workplace' or a 'work-based' ministry. The confusion arises because of the way in which, to many people, 'ministry' is a series of clearly defined tasks largely corresponding to those set out in the Odinal and which are, in the main, activities concerned with the building up of the life of the local Church. To speak then of the workplace as the focus of an ordained ministry which does not seem to be expressed in terms even remotely similar to such activities inevitably leads to misunderstanding and confusion in both lay and clerical minds. It is also true that this situation has sometimes been exacerbated by some NSMs being unwilling or unable to give a clearer account of their work in terms of how it relates to 'ministry' as people have traditionally understood it.

At one level there has already been a major change during the past quarter of a century in the way ministry is conceived and, as was pointed out in the previous chapter, NSMs as a bridge between clergy and lay, could play an important rôle in the recovery of ministry for the whole Church. Unfortunately even where there has been a wider understanding of ministry as the concern of all (what has sometimes been called an 'every-member ministry'), the tasks of ministry have still tended to be thought of in what might be called crypto-clerical terms, tasks predominantly associated with the operation of the local church and its immediate concerns. Such ministries can be manifold, from elders to house-group leaders, from home visitors to the ministry of welcome which greets visitors at the front door of the church. Though this church-centredness may make for the smoother running of the life of the local church, it inevitably tends to make the life of the local church into an end in itself, rather than seeing that the church exists to serve something other than itself.

According to the Nicene Creed the Church has four hallmarks: that it is One, Holy, Catholic and Apostolic. Of the four the last, *apostolic*, has long struck me as being at one and the same time the most biblical and also the most neglected. It has been said that the Church stands in relation to mission in much the same way as does fire to burning. Though every institution needs sufficient attention to be able to maintain its life, Christian experience has often been of a Church in which the institutional tail has wagged the dog. Mission has often been regarded as merely one among other concerns and, not unusually, one to which we give attention only when other things have been attended to. The contrast between that and, say, the sense of purpose expressed in the Acts of the Apostles, is enormous. But what is the mission of the Church?

There are two models which have been predominant in the history of the Church. The first is that of 'in-gathering', essentially seeing the task of the Christian as being that of drawing men and women out of the world into the fellowship of a particular society. In such a model the chief emphasis has been upon breaking with the cultural context in which people live and accepting the culture of the Church. Considerable energies have been given to this model and they have occasioned acts of heroism and commitment for which countless people throughout the world have had cause to be enormously grateful. The missionary societies in particular were often brought into being and sustained for long years by such an understanding of mission and many people responded to their vision and gave themselves to it.

The second model (which has now, interestingly, tended to become the prevalent model within many missionary societies) has been much more concerned with 'out-going' into the world to work within the prevailing culture and seeking so to direct it that it accords with God's will. In such a model the Church exists to serve the world, and its members see themselves as akin to the yeast or salt of which Jesus spoke.

In practice neither model has probably operated in pure form. Nevertheless the influence of the former has been considerable, as a consequence of which there has developed a powerful mentality within the Church which has tended to think of ministry as essentially consequent upon it. My contention is that we need to place further emphasis upon the latter, not to offset the influence of the former but to complement it. It is in this area of mission that I am convinced we need to understand what a 'workplace ministry' might be.

I once went into the book department of a major store. As I might have expected the range of books on offer could largely be classified as 'popular' – paperbacks of many kind. The only religious books I could see were some Bibles and Prayer Books, all of which were actually inaccessible to customers because they were locked away in a glass-fronted display cabinet. It seemed to me a parable of how many people in our society, within and without the churches, see religion: something special, indeed often very special indeed, but ideally removed from the ordinariness of the world and only invoked on the rare but particular occasions when needed.

Many Christians think along similar lines. Their 'church-life' is something quite apart from the rest and to encounter the vicar in the workplace would feel most inappropriate. Indeed as an industrial chaplain the moments when I most encountered resistance or misunderstanding were usually occasioned by church people who just couldn't see what they knew of religion had to do with the sort of place in which they worked. It was almost as if they worshipped more than one god. There was first of all the god of the home and leisure time who was prayed to and worshipped on Sundays. There was also however another god whose domain was the public world of work and the painful realities of economic life. This god was never worshipped explicitly but clearly had the means of extracting service from his adherents and generally seemed to give them what they wanted in return. From time to time I encountered men and women who really did appear to embody such a polytheist divide within themselves.

Industry and commerce do of course feel as if they embody values which are far distant from those of the Christian faith and I do not underestimate the struggles of those who seek to serve just one God within them. I equally understand why many Christians look upon their work as some kind of necessary evil and see church as the embodiment of what is most good, to which they might well wish to give of themselves to a considerable degree. But neither can I avoid the feeling that such ambivalence towards the world of work is ultimately rooted in a mistaken, or inadequate, understanding of God and his purposes in creation, as well as an inadequate understanding of how the Church stands in relation to them.

For such reasons I would want to express considerable anxiety about the dominance of the 'in-gathering' model of mission for it ever so easily leads to a division being made between various territories over which particular gods seem to be allowed sovereignty. This recalls, for me an important, perhaps the most important, theme of the Old Testament: the kingship or active rule of God.

The idea of God as the ruler of Israel represented a major theological development from an earlier tradition in which God was recognised and worshipped simply as creator. A key passage in this respect in Exodus 6.2f:

'God said to Moses, "I am the Lord. I appeared to Abraham,
Isaac, and Jacob as God Almighty; but I did not let myself be
known to them by my name, the Lord".'

The distinction here is between God as *El Shaddai*, a name
associated with God as the all-powerful creator and sustain-
er of all, there to be worshipped and feared even when in
contact with the patriarchs, and *Jahweh*, the God who
enters into a close and intimate relationship with a
particular people.

The Old Testament is witness to the development of this
religious idea and its consequences for a people. Just what it
meant to speak of God actively leading his people, preparing a land for them, vanquishing their foes – all the characteristic actions of a great earthly ruler, had to be worked out
in practical terms. In so many respects the ups and downs of
the life of Israel, a history often complex and messy, can
legitimately be compared to that of our own times as people
struggle to discover meaning and purpose in the face of
conflicting gods in the form of competing ideologies and
economic systems.

Somewhat ironically the greatest step forward in the
process of understanding came about as a result of what, to
all intents and purposes, was Israel's greatest tragedy – the
exile into Babylon. The nation was devastated, the temple
destroyed and the people led away into slavery. No wonder
the Psalmist could write:

'By the rivers of Babylon we sat down and wept
as we remembered Zion . . .'

(Psalm 137.1)

Yet out of that tragedy of immense proportions emerged
three writers whose vision and hope was to transform
human thinking about God from that day to this. Jeremiah,
Ezekiel and the so-called 'Second Isaiah' (author of chapters
40–55) expressed three themes in particular which relate
directly to the theme of the Kingly rule of God: its judgement, its universal nature, and its future expression.

The relationship between God's will and the morality of the people of Israel found expression in the dictates of the law books and their related rituals. Earlier prophetic writing referred to this as it called for the pattern of life within the nation to do justice to the enormity of their particular vocation as God's people, a relationship spelled out in terms of social justice and generosity:

> 'The Lord has told you mortals what is good,
> and what it is that the Lord requires of you:
> only to act justly, to love loyalty,
> to walk humbly with your God.'
>
> (Micah 6.8)

To this was added a powerful awareness that such a moral view linked up with the fate of the nation, in which forgiveness was offered provided the nation abandoned its former ways and renewed itself:

> 'Yet even, now says the Lord,
> turn back to me wholeheartedly
> with fasting, weeping, and mourning.
> Rend your hearts and not your garments,
> and turn back to the Lord your God,
> for he is gracious and compassionate,
> long-suffering and ever constant,
> ready always to relent when he threatens disaster.'
>
> (Joel 2.12f)

The exile forced the nation to rethink its relationship with God. The judgement they were now experiencing was far more radical than they could have imagined possible:

> 'These are the words of the Lord of Hosts the God of Israel:
> . . . when I brought your forefathers out of Egypt, I gave them no instructions or commands about whole-offerings or sacrifice. What I did command them was this: Obey me, and I shall be your God and you will be my people. You must conform to all my commands, if you are to prosper.
> But they did not listen; they paid no heed, and persisted in their own plans with evil and stubborn hearts; they turned

their backs and not their faces to me, from the day when your forefathers left Egypt until now. Again and again I sent to them all my servants the prophets; but instead of listening and paying heed to me, they in their stubbornness proved even more wicked than their forefathers. . . . This is the nation who did not obey the Lord their God or accept correction. Truth has perished; it is heard no more on their lips.'

(Jeremiah 7.21a, 22–6, 28)

Now in exile they were experiencing the consequences of still regarding *Jahweh* as *El Shaddai*, failing in the most practical of ways to recognise the active ruling presence of God in their midst. Now in exile they were to discover too just what it really meant to speak of God as their King, and what this implied for their pattern of life after their return from exile in terms of unity of worship and the demands of social justice and righteousness.

In exile, far from Jerusalem and its Temple, the seat of God's presence, they discerned his continuing presence among them. That God could be known outside Israel and far from the Temple, made some of them begin to realise that he was not limited to national boundaries, and that if he was their king, so also might he perhaps be the true king of the whole earth:

'Who has raised up from the east
one greeted by victory wherever he goes,
making nations his subjects
and overthrowing their kings?
He scatters them with his sword like dust
and with his bow like chaff driven before the wind;
he puts them to flight and passes on unscathed,
swifter than any traveller on foot.
Whose work is this, who has brought it to pass?
Who has summoned the generations from the beginning?
I, the Lord, was with the first of them,
and I am with those who come after.'

(Isaiah 41.2–4)

This universalist vision was linked together with a belief in the vocation of Israel as the mediator of God's presence:

> 'I have formed you, and destined you to be a light for peoples.'

> (Isaiah 49.8)

but no longer could God be regarded as their private possession. The Second Isaiah in particular was to speak of Cyrus, King of the Persians, as God's 'anointed', a term previously reserved for the king of Israel.

The third element in the writings of the exilic and post-exilic prophets concerns the future, not merely the fact of the restoration but beyond it to the quality of life in the restored land of Israel:

> 'You, my people, will know that I am the Lord when I open your graves and bring you up from them. Then I shall put my spirit into you and you will come to life, and I shall settle you on your own soil, and you will know that I the Lord have spoken and I shall act.'

> (Ezekiel 37.13f)

It is not however merely restoration but a new departure:

> 'The days are coming, says the Lord, when I shall establish a new covenant with the people of Israel and Judah. It will not be like the covenant I made with their forefathers when I took them by the hand to lead them out of Egypt, a covenant they broke, though I was patient with them, says the Lord. For this is the covenant I shall establish with the Israelites after those days, says the Lord: I shall set my law within them, writing it on their hearts; I shall be their God, and they will be my people.'

> (Jeremiah 31.31ff)

We might say then what we are offered here is a vision of only one God whose domain is the whole world, not just the 'religious'. A God who is to be served in terms of justice and righteousness and who longs for the establishment of right-eousness in the life of the nation. That nation exists both to live out that vision in its life but also to be a herald of it in the whole world. The subsequent history of Israel may never have realised it, but it remains a compelling vision!

It is against such a background of thought that we need to see and understand the first words which Mark puts into the mouth of Jesus, and which serve as a kind of manifesto for his mission ahead: 'The time has arrived; the kingdom of God is upon you. Repent, and believe the gospel.' (1.15).

Luke adds to them his account of Jesus' preaching in the synagogue in Nazareth:

> 'The spirit of the Lord is upon me
> because he has anointed me;
> he has sent me to announce good news to the poor,
> to proclaim release for prisoners
> and recovery of sight for the blind;
> to let the broken victims go free,
> to proclaim the year of the Lord's favour.'

(Luke 4.18f)

One of the areas in which almost all New Testament scholars are united is in their recognition that the theme of the 'Kingdom of God' could be said to be the hallmark of Jesus' teaching (it occurs no fewer than 108 times in the first three gospels). It has been suggested that the actual Aramaic phrase which would have been used by Jesus was *malkuta dishemaya*, the literal meaning of which is 'kingdom of the heavens' referring not to some other-worldly realm but to the very being of God, a reality too holy to be named. In Matthew's gospel the writer in fact prefers to speak of the 'Kingdom of heaven' to describe what Mark and Luke both call the 'Kingdom of God', though it is clear that the meaning of both is the same – the present and active ruling power of God.

The essence of Jesus' teaching is that the active ruling power of God is an all-embracing reality that cannot be halted. At various times he seems to have spoken of it as already present, albeit hidden, and then at others in terms of its in-breaking perhaps accompanied by calamitous eschatological events. Jesus called men and women to make themselves ready for the life of the Kingdom and saw his own mighty works as signs of its imminent arrival. Evil was being overcome, God's victory was upon them and, for the poor in particular, there would be a great overturning of worldly values whereby the least would be made great by God. True worth and value were about to be recognised, and wherever Jesus brought healing and life, there the truth of the kingdom was already being experienced.

In the famous incident when Jesus told his hearers to 'render unto Caesar the things which are Caesar's and to God the things which are God's' (Luke 20.19–26) he was pointing beyond the earthly wisdom of his interlocutors, which was seeking to catch him out, to a vision of the world in which everything is recognised as God's (even Caesar!), and all, finally, to be judged by him.

It is possible to draw together some conclusions about Jesus' teaching of the Kingdom of God.

(1) The Kingdom is God's gift, promised and ratified in the new covenant. It can be proclaimed, preached and announced (e.g. Lk. 9.60; Matt. 4.23; Lk. 8.1); it may be received and entered (e.g. Mk. 10.15; Lk. 18.24f); at the same time it has not yet come in its fullness and people are summoned to seek it assiduously (Matt. 6.33), to make sacrifices for it (Matt. 5.29f). Clearly it can be lost. The rich, for example, may well discover it is beyond them (Matt. 19.23f; Mk. 10.23ff) and there is a sharp element of judgement, closely related to moral action, involved in the issue of who may and who may not enter (Matt. 13.18–30; 25 passim).

(2) The reality of the Kingdom is such that it can almost be described in terms of being in accord with God's will, something stressed by the parallelism of the Lord's Prayer (Matt. 5.10):

> 'your kingdom come,
> your will be done,
> on earth as in heaven.'

Here the sovereignty of God, the active rule of God, is identified as compliance with God's will in such a way as to suggest that whenever and wherever the will of God is done, there the Kingdom of God, the active ruling power of God, is being served.

(3) The Kingdom in its fullness belongs to the future, and its realisation will be the work of God, though Jesus foresaw his own death having a major part to play in its inauguration. In this way his own identity and that of the Kingdom are inextricably bound together.

It is, I believe, possible to draw together the prophetic vision of the Old Testament and the teaching of Jesus about the Kingdom of God in such a way as to relate it to the theme of ministry. There is first of all an emphasis upon the sovereignty of God as something alive and active, something to which the Church as the community of God's people is called both to embody and also act as herald. Second, there is a clear sense that the Church, as Israel before, needs to recognise that God is not limited to a realm labelled 'religion' but is Lord of all the earth, a Lord served whenever and wherever the will of God is being done. The third is a recognition that the Church exists to serve the whole of God's realm and not merely pull people out of the world into an exclusive club.

Such an understanding will just not permit us to divide the world up into various, apparently autonomous, realms. It serves to remind the churches that although we may at times like to imagine there is a divide (note the astonishing invitation in the Rite A Communion Service: 'Let us pray for the Church and for the World'!), such a view clashes markedly with the concept of the universality of God's active ruling presence emerging from the exilic experience of Israel and reflected in Jesus' insistence that the whole earth and its people's belong to God.

Nor can it realistically be maintained that the Church alone does the will of God, for although in some Christian preaching the 'world' is held to be the repository of the

spiritual enemy and consequently quite incapable of anything good, most Christian theology has come to recognise
that at least some people, some of the time, do things which
accord with God's will. Once this is allowed, in however
qualified a form, the Kingdom is at once extended beyond
the boundaries of the Church.

We might say then that the Church has a clearly ordained
role as a community whose existence is bound up with the
proclamation of the active ruling presence of God. It is not
only a herald of the Kingdom and its future, but also called
to be a sacrament of its fulfilment by virtue of its relationship to God in Christ who alone can sustain it as such.
Once however, we have begun to recognise that the scope
and dimensions of the Kingdom are not exhausted within
the boundaries of our discussion about the Church, we need
to discover ways in which it then becomes possible for
the Church also to serve as herald to the Kingdom beyond
itself, and it is in terms of this particular 'ministry' that we
can begin to see what a 'workplace ministry' might be.

Although a great deal of ecclesiology has happily maintained a distinction between church and world, in practice
most Church members have never drawn too sharp a line in
demarcation between them. Even in those denominations
which have most explicitly claimed a world-denying sec-
tarian identity it has been hard save for a few determined
individuals to maintain any kind of credible consistency.
Most Christians recognise sufficient reality to know that
they are within the world, and that, on the whole, they are
happy to accept its benefits. Nevertheless a mental construction is largely accepted, even if conveniently laid aside when
appropriate, which conceives of church and world in
opposition.

At the popular level, and in diluted form, in ordinary
Church life this is reflected in the distaste for clerical involvement in the practicalities of political life. Given that
most lay people recognise themselves too compromised and
involved with the world they project onto their clergy a

necessity for being unworldly (though the English in particular do not like them over other-worldly). Because clergy ultimately represent God, political life in particular, with its necessary compromises and scheming, is deemed to be beyond the domain of God which is still regarded as essentially characterised by simplicity and purity.

All non-stipendiary ministers, whether in secular employment or not, depend on the economic system of the 'world' for their livelihood. In practice of course so also do all stipendiary ministers – the Church Commissioners have a most positive doctrine of the world and the worth of its investments! NSMs in secular employment however can be said to have a more direct involvement both by virtue of their being paid by a 'secular' rather than a 'sacred' institution, and also because their energies are being directed day-by-day, as with almost all lay men and women, towards the better functioning of the 'world', whatever theology they might incidentally happen to profess.

The presence of an ordained minister in a place of work can have fascinating effects. The visit of an industrial chaplain to a department is not unlike the visit of a vicar to a home: it will be short-lived and occasion unusual but temporary behaviour. The permanent ordained minister is a different creature altogether. At first there are inevitable comments indicative of some kind of adaptation but eventually these give way more or less to a return to normality. From time to time they discover that requests come to them simply because they are ordained ministers – people come to chat who might not otherwise, there is the occasional conversation about how someone should set about getting married or having their baby baptised and so on. In this respect the NSM represents the local church. Sometimes she or he will even be asked to play a ministerial role for a specific individual (funerals are a classic example of this) though largely NSMs have been educated and are more than happy to direct people towards their own clergy, something which has helped reduce mistrust on the part of parish clergy who fear that in some way an NSM might be 'poaching'.

What is most interesting is that once the novelty of having an ordained minister has worn off, the life of that particular department or area really does assume much the same air it always did. Mary may have been ordained but she is obviously still Mary. Frank may now be a priest, but he has not stopped being Frank. The sort of silliness which often characterises a workplace when an industrial chaplain appears, such as endless apologies about bad language and giggles about the posters on the wall (and against which some industrial chaplains react by endeavouring to show how bad their own language can be) largely just does not happen to NSMs.

The reasons for this may be found in the consequences of generations of experience both of the Church through its clergy, and also its theology through the Church. From my own experience I have come to believe that many people outside the membership of the churches (and also indeed a good number within) regard the clergy essentially as those who do what they do because they are quite unable to do anything else – well-meaning perhaps, but effeminate fun-spoilers all the same, and of whom one has low expectations which are rarely exceeded. Behind the clergy can be seen the Church of which many people in our country take not the blindest bit of notice, and who when they do, because of items of news, have their worst suspicions confirmed. Just as the clergy are regarded as fun-spoilers, so they are taken as typical of the whole institution, and this would go as much for so-called lively charismatic churches as it does for the traditional 'established churches. Somehow or other the idea has been spread abroad that those who belong to the churches see themselves as superior to others.

In actual fact of course the theological presuppositions of ecclesiology assume precisely this. It is often consciously tempered but that it requires such a tempering is to my mind evidence of its essential truth. When I have preached that

those who come to church do so because we are sinners,
even though there has been a grudging acknowledgement
that this is of course so in terms of theology, I have been
profoundly conscious of a considerable resistance to the
idea. It is extraordinarily difficult to preach about the
Pharisee and the Publican or the Workers in the Vineyard,
stories with an extremely sharp cutting edge, and be heard.

So when non-Churchgoers manifest a degree of ag-
gression towards those who go it is amongst other things a
mirroring of the way in which the Church looks upon those
who do not attend church – the 'world'.

It is however also something more. For although many
(actually, by far and away, most) people feel little compul-
sion to attend any church service, even at Christmas, what is
surprising is that so many of them nevertheless still give
expression to something deep within themselves that requires some kind of religious or quasi-religious recognition.
Considerable numbers persist in seeking baptism or a
church wedding and an occasion of death has now become
the likely moment of encounter for most people with an
ordained minister. That this is so distresses many clergy,
though (provided clergy and willing to do some demanding
theological work) these could quite legitimately be regarded
as a prime time for their ministry. What people are respond-
ing to within themselves may well be dismissed by some as
folk religion but at least it is something do with a recognition that the Church has some kind of representative role,
a holding brief, for ultimate things.

I have long maintained that the most important moment
in the process of baptism occurs when the vicarage door is
opened to an enquirer. If they are at once welcomed and
received, something good and true has been communicated
about those ultimate things Christians allegedly profess. If
an enquiry is greeted gruffly because it is clearly regarded as
an intrusion, or with a series of questions designed to
unearth some possible obstacle to the baptism (e.g. 'Where
actually do you live – in this parish or another?'), or if the

enquirer is made to feel that she or he is being presented with an assault course as the condition of baptism (because they are made to feel that in not coming to church they will have to earn the baptism by suffering for it), then no matter how pleasant the minister is subsequently, the damage has been done and he really has in that moment communicated the true nature of his feelings and beliefs, and they will not have any resonance within those who have looked to him for them.

It is much the same for clergy in the workplace. I used to be puzzled by why it was, given that people clearly felt such ambivalence about clergy, they were often so welcoming to me as an industrial chaplain. I am now convinced it was because in spite of people's experience of the Church and its theology, they still look (albeit usually unconsciously and, I am beginning to fear, less and less) to the ordained person as a person representative of something ultimate, and that this flows out of some deep inner need for acceptance and recognition. But this is not merely a personal affirmation, an acceptance of individuals. It is also about acceptance and recognition being given to the world of work, to the 'world' in which men and women actually dwell and to which they often feel a considerable degree of commitment.

Of course there are bad things in the world – no one would deny that, but there are many more good things. In the world people grow, fall in love, celebrates, produce children, find opportunities to relate to others, contribute something to the common good, laugh and cry. And they do all these things quite spontaneously without any need for legitimation by the Church. Generations of emphasis upon original sin and the fallen state of humankind has primarily served to warp the mind of the Church, one of the principal features of which is an inability to see the essential goodness of creation, and that made in the image and likeness of God human beings can come to know extraordinary degrees of joy.

I recall some years ago being profoundly moved by

an article written by Bernard Levin on the film *Close Encounters of the Third Kind*:

> '... the final effect of the film is to send us out with an extraordinary exalted feeling, of the kind that we get before any work of art that expresses – as all true art does and must – the sense of order and harmony with its irreducible core of mystery, in the universe. In other words, we emerge with the feeling that not only the film, but the universe, has got the answer right.'
>
> (Levin 1979, p. 258)

Too often Christians have seemed only interested in finding fault with the world, in seeing things which are wrong, instead of concentrating on signs of what some of the early Fathers of the Church call the original righteousness of creation.

There is of course a darker side to being human – no one reflecting upon some of the events of this century could possibly deny that, but there is an equally dark side to being Christian:

> 'We are at fault in not slaying them. Rather we allow them to live freely in our midst despite all their murdering, cursing, blaspheming, lying and defaming ...
>
> What shall we Christians do with this rejected and condemned people, the Jews? Since they live among us, we dare not tolerate their conduct, now that we are aware of their lying and reviling and blaspheming ...
>
> First, to set fire to their synagogues or schools and to cover with dirt whatever will not burn so that no man will ever see a stone or cinder of them. This is to be done in honour of our Lord and Christendom, so that God might see that we are Christians, and do not condone or knowingly tolerate such public lying, cursing, and blaspheming of his Son and of his Christians ...
>
> Second, I advise that their houses be razed and destroyed. For they pursue in them the same aims as in their synagogues.'

These words were not written by a Nazi consumed by anti-semitism, but by Martin Luther, and many people searching out the roots of anti-semitism have again and again found themselves laying much of the blame upon the Church, even upon the gospels themselves. It is a realisation that has brought many Christians to a deeper recognition and penitence for much that has been amiss in their tradition. This is not to say the Church as a human institution is worse than others (though it has been responsible for a great deal of harm in the world over many centuries), but simply to recognise that just as it shares in the human lot in terms of its darker side, the whole world and not just the Church can also manifest the lighter side, the essential goodness of creation. Sometimes, on the contrary, the 'world' has been well ahead of the Church in terms of its track record, and at the present time many people looking at the way the Church behaves with regard to women conclude that the 'world' is a long way ahead in promoting the values and worth of the Kingdom of God.

I am more than ever convinced of just how important it is for representatives of the Church, representatives of the ultimate, to be wholly inolved with and in the activities of the whole creation. For reasons suggested above, a 'chaplaincy' model has only limited possibilities. Far better in a workplace is someone who can manifest day in and day out her or his commitment to the world of work and show that it matters ultimately, that it matters to God.

Theologically of course, work as such has been viewed as a consequence of the fall (Gen. 3.17ff). Some people do not like their work and may indeed feel it is a curse. But for many others it is no such thing at all. Work is for them something essentially positive and good. Not only does it provide them with a shape to their lives but allows them to contribute to society (at the very least through their taxes), and for many people is the place and activity in and through which they give their very best.

I recall two conversations during a visit round a Copper

Works in Leeds. The men were working on adjacent machines though, because of the noise, fortunately neither could hear my conversation with the other. I asked each in turn what they did (even though their work was obviously identical I had already discovered that it was a good opening line!). The first replied that he cut and bent tubes! It was an accurate if not exactly stimulating reply, for his work consisted of feeding copper tubes into a machine which bent and cut the tubes to a required length. In moving on to his neighbour I suppose I was anticipating a similar response; after all what more could you add about what appeared to me to be soul-destroying work? Imagine then my surprise when he replied 'I make submarines'! Nor was he jesting for, as he told me, the tubes he was bending and cutting were being used in submarine construction and he liked to think of himself as participating in that whole process. To this day when I see a submarine on television I think of that conversation and picture him pointing his grandchildren to the television and telling them: 'Grandad made that!'

For this man, and many others, work represents something good in itself, not just a means to an end in terms of money. Statistics reveal just how many men in particular die within the immediate period after retirement. Loss of work is often the loss of a great part of their self. This was powerfully illustrated for me when I encountered one of the Little Brothers of Jesus. As a member of that particular religious order living in the poorest parts of our cities he had been well trained, an iron discipline being knocked into him from the moment he entered the novitiate. Each day in addition to their having to work they were obliged to spend a minimum of an hour in silent prayer in the chapel in the attic, say the daily office and attend Mass. It was not an easy life and those who have met them have usually been very impressed by their commitment and their determination. For me all this turned to shock and considerable distress when I heard that this particular brother had been made redundant (this was in the early 1980s when unemployment was at its highest and there was little chance of him getting another job), for the effect of redundancy upon him was quite terrifying. He found he couldn't face getting up in the morning and he was overcome by a lethargy and sense of worthlessness which his many years of training and monastic experience could do nothing to alleviate. Only a year or so later when he finally managed to get another job did his self-esteem, together with his ability to get up and pray, return.

I do not want to romanticise work. For many people it is still dangerous and manifestly unjustly rewarded. Yet people still want to work and it seems clear that doing so is one way in which we can work together with God by engaging in purposeful activity, a sign perhaps that we are made for a particular end which is to be creative. Christians may well be critical of the world of technology but its creative potential cannot be denied. Human achievements may include the atomic bomb, but equally they include the use of radiation for helping overcome cancer; there may well be serious problems of pollution to be faced but modern chemicals can also save the lives of sick children.

The presence of an NSM in a place of work is the literal embodiment of the most positive thing the Church could want to say about the world. There an ordained minister seeks to serve the Kingdom of God by engaging with others in purposeful activity, a part of a huge network of people the world over.

Such a vision finds perfect expression in the celebration of the Eucharist. If we pause and consider the gifts of bread and wine brought up to the altar in the Eucharist we can perhaps see that we are offering considerably more than the mere species there presented. The bread for example, probably began its existence as seed planted some time back, perhaps half way across the world on the great Canadian prairies. Throughout the long hot summer it grew tended by farmers with their powerful agricultural sprays. Eventually it was harvested and the grain transported to a depot from

whence it began its long journey across Canada toward the
coast and transfer onto a ship. Already by this stage it has
been handled by a good many people, and many more have
been involved in the processes of buying and selling, the
world of international finance. After crossing the Atlantic it
is transported to a mill for grinding and preparation, before
making yet another journey to a bakery before it begins its
journey to the shop. Our own purchase is but the last in a
long line which has involved many hundreds of people
engaged in purposeful activity half way across the world.
When it finally appears in church on a Sunday morning it
has already come a very long way and it comes representing
all those people and all those processes who together have
made it into bread to be offered to God on the altar. The
same could go for the wine or the vessels in which they are
contained. We do not merely offer to God bread and wine
but the whole earth and all its workings, though the point
can be made much more powerfully if real bread is used, and
even more if it has been baked by members of the congregation or the wine is a genuine 'home brew'. In each
celebration of the Eucharist the whole world of work, the
world of purposeful human activity, is offered to God.

Many people coming to the Old Testament for the first
time express a degree of dismay at what appears to be so
'unspiritual'. There are huge chunks of law and page after
page of history, and although there are of course passages of
great beauty and profundity in the psalms such obviously
'religious' writings are somehow very subordinate within
the whole to the other material. Yet to the Hebrews a sharp
line of differentiation between sacred and secular, between
life and religion was almost unknown. God is known and
served through the matter of fact everyday activities of life,
and is largely encountered not in the special experiences of
'misty mountain tops', the temple or synagogue but in the
midst of the ordinary. And it is within the ordinary that God
is to be served today too. In this respect not only do
NSMs embody God's presence in the 'world' but they may

also be seen by the Church as a whole as role models of how God is to be served. Christians often want help with living out their faith in and through their work or in the life and activities of their local community. The NSM must recall that one of the obligations of their ordination promises is to make themselves examples for others to follow. It is no small matter but it cannot be evaded.

So it is clear that the whole world is the place where God is to be served, his will sought and co-operation to be given. No doubt many people presented with such a view would agree – in theory! The problems arise when the world of work is recognised as being a murky world full of compromises and an intrinsic set of values that inevitably clash with those of the Christian faith. Is it then possible to speak of working purposefully with God?

Some years ago I spent some time with a businessman, also a Christian, working in one of the depressed areas. He was the managing director of a small manufacturing company which he had begun in 1969, and we were discussing how it was that he had managed to stay in business during the late 1970s and early 1980s when the effects of the economic recession were at their height, and when many of his competitors had gone out of business. He replied that there had been more than a few times when survival had been possible only by sailing very close to the wind ethically. By this he meant payments and gifts to buyers and others so as to secure business. 'We put them down as insurance premiums' he said, and in one sense that is exactly what they were. The alternative would have been closure and the loss, not only of his own, but the jobs of those who worked for him, the majority of whom were the only bread winner in their family and with little hope of alternative employment.

Some Christians would maintain that, faced with what they would regard as bribery, he ought to have preferred closure than succumb to such pressure. Others, when I have discussed the principle with them, have suggested that he ought to have gone over the heads of those to whom he made payments and reported them to their companies. But how appropriate in terms of ethics are either of these?

The former has the virtue of perfectionism. The Christian can wash his hands of the dirty world and although he goes out of business he retains a powerful sense of his own integrity. No doubt too he will have to endure a great deal of loss in the process. But what of his responsibilities as an employer, and indirectly, his responsibilities toward the families of his employees? Do not they have a claim on his conscience? And even were he to have gone ahead and accepted the loss of business and consequent closure, would there not have been a competitor waiting to step into the breach and provide the necessary 'payments and gifts'? Such competitors might even rub their hands together with glee, send a contribution to the support of the Full Gospel Businessmens Fellowship and long for more conversions among their competitors! Are Christians to flee the world and leave it to the devil?

The latter option, that of reporting buyers to their bosses, (apart from the dubious moral principle of pointing out the sins of others), is born more of naïvety than moral concern. Senior management are not stupid; they know what sort of system the world of business and commerce is, and whilst they might be obliged to act in certain circumstances, the final effect of such an action might well be a loss of business anyway. A new buyer might automatically prefer to deal with others less likely to force their moral views on his new bosses.

No one, least of all the particular person who first told me this story, would pretend that the alternative to these 'obviously moral' approaches is easy to live with. How easy is it to measure 'payments and gifts' against the jobs and livelihoods of those employed? It is an extremely grey moral area and Christians who prefer to see everything simply in terms of black and white are not necessarily those with perfect eyesight.

In the end my friend decided that as a Christian employer

he owed a great debt to his employees (it was not of course pure altruism – he also kept his own job and business!) and bear the cost of his moral choice within himself. Sunday by Sunday when he confessed his sins in church, he did so full well aware that he was caught up in things from which he couldn't wriggle free and which, of necessity, he knew he would be confessing again next time. Even so is not that preferable to abandoning responsibility in favour of a doubtful self-righteousness?

When we offer our gifts at the altar on a Sunday morning we are not presenting to God our righteousness, the fruits of our virtue. The economic and commercial world which has enabled the bread and wine, not to mention the money accompanying them, to be placed there, is compromised and messy much of the time, and we offer that to God too. The priestly work of the people of God is not to bring the fruits of their perfection but their need of redemption and whilst this should not be used to legitimate any confusion between what is right and what is wrong, neither should it be used by any to imagine that they are somehow worthy to be at the Eucharist. We all come as sinners, and we bring with us a sinful world which cries out for healing.

Non-stipendiary ministers know full well from their own involvement, their own complicity with the sinful structures of unredeemed humankind, that their priestly task is to present such an offering to God. Often, as with the man mentioned above, they will recognise that they do this with a heavy heart precisely because they know how caught up in the web of sin the world of work can be, but nevertheless they can do it with hope. Although not exactly what was meant by Paul, they might well apply to themselves the words from his letter to the Romans:

> 'I discover this principle, then: that when I want to do right, only wrong is within my reach. In my inmost self I delight in the law of God, but I perceive in my outward actions a different law, fighting against the law that my mind approves, and making me a prisoner under the law of sin

which controls my conduct. Wretched creature that I am, who is there to rescue me from this state of death? Who but God? Thanks be to him through Jesus Christ our Lord!'

(Rom. 7.21–25a)

Of course stipendiary ministers too are caught up in the sinful structures of humankind but the NSM, because of her obvious and visible presence in the workplace, is a clearer representative of the Church and of God also present within the complexity of the world of work with all its compromises. She is a resource to other Christians simply by her presence, and even more by her ability to acknowledge openly the extent to which she, like them, is bound by constraints. My experience as a chaplain to industry revealed just how many people experience considerable guilt in the face of the enormous pressures and compromises they feel obliged to make. There is an important market here for every Christian minister.

This is one way then in which we might say the Kingdom of God is looked and longed for, and for which the NSM can be an effective and powerful role model. It is however not quite the same as that process of endeavouring to make our life align itself with the will of God which we saw above as one of the central elements of the later Hebrew understanding of the Kingdom. A positive doctrine of compromise may well be necessary in one area of life but are there not limits beyond which compromise is quite unacceptable? What is to be done when that limit is reached and the demands of the Kingdom of God are recognised as being in direct conflict with the existing order not merely in uneasy compromise?

The commercial and industrial sectors of life have long been recognised as highly politicised; in recent years many other occupations have found themselves much more influenced by and bound to contentious political choices than formerly. Doctors and school teachers (favourite occupations of NSMs) together with a whole variety of others have come to see that their work is part of the way the nation orders its life and that to have a concern for that ordering is not something limited to the ballot box every four or five years. Democracy is more than a mere surrendering to others the right to decide what is to be done.

I suspect that many Christians find the antics of politicians and the actuality of political life distasteful. Because the majority of members of the Church of England, have tended to belong to the relatively secure middle-class which has largely no need to engage in corporate political action or seek the security of trade unions, it has been somewhat inevitable that the majority have tended to support a *laissez faire* approach, characteristic of the post-war Conservative party before 1979.

As a consequence of and in reaction to the policies of successive governments since 1979, this *laissez faire* attitude has come more widely to be recognised as not in itself sufficient. Issues such as the environment, health care and public sector policy as a whole are of great concern to many people and there seems to be less trust than hitherto in the politicians charged with their ordering. The subservience of all policy to economics is a doctrine which Christians in particular will struggle to swallow. In consequence there has been a grudging and reluctant recognition even by the churches that life is becoming more and more politicised.

At the same time there remains the deep-seated prejudice against the clergy becoming over-involved in political matters referred to above. Their representative role is apparently seriously compromised in the eyes of many if they are seen to be taking sides in a political and economic context. Sometimes too, the history of clerical involvement in politics suggests that often they are an example of 'innocents abroad' and that most clergy would do well to speak as little as they must about complex matters which will not be advanced by well-intended but muddled nonsense from the pulpit or parish magazine.

Nevertheless the biblical understanding of the Kingdom of God demands a commitment to and care for peace and justice – that understanding of Shalom which is not merely the absence of conflict but the presence of justice and wholeness within a society. Part of that involves a commitment to the poor and outcast such as characterised Jesus' own ministry, the manifesto for which he presented in the synagogue in Nazareth. Some writers such as Bishop David Sheppard in this country and many others abroad (where issues of power and justice are much sharper) have come to speak of a divine bias to the poor. A society, such as ours, which is largely very wealthy will of course find such an idea extremely difficult and unattractive, but that must go for a fair amount of material in the New Testament dealing with money. Somehow we have a feeling that God must be equally accessible to all. That is true, but God's demand of repentance as the key to the Kingdom is one with it. For that reason the Church as the agents of proclamation of the Kingdom must persist in summoning the world to repentance and this means, amongst other things, a summons to political, economic and social repentance.

This is not to mean that Christians must constantly be dreaming up grand plans or think that by involvig themselves in international social issues they have thereby done all that is asked of them as the people of God. Far more important is the work of striving to forward the cause of the Kingdom in that small part of the world each inhabits. There must be times of compromise and also times when compromise is unacceptable, the principle criterion of which will be the fate of the poorest.

Simply by being an employee, the NSM is caught up in the political processes of society. How she deals with the political issues involved in her work will say a great deal about how she sees and understands the Kingdom of God and her decisions act as a role model for those other Christians who find themselves both bewildered yet certain that somehow they have to persist with expressing their faith in and through the economic and political mechanisms in which they find themselves.

A further function of the NSM is that of recognising and affirming those who do not have any Christian commitment, who may not even believe in God, but whose lives manifest a clear commitment to the causes of peace and justice. They may not be able to acknowledge a God but in so far as they do his will they are already becoming part of his Kingdom. This would go too for the important task of recognising and affirming those whose work is healing. So much Christian writing on the subject of healing has tended to suggest that the healing activity of God is confined to the sometimes bizarre activities of self-styled 'healers', forgetful of the undramatic 'miracles' that happen every day in hospitals, dental surgeries, opticians, consulting rooms, probation service offices and so on. Healing has been around longer than the charismatic movement, there were healers long before Jesus!

Where the NSM differs from her lay Christian colleagues is her visible representative role – she embodies the Church, she embodies God, in a way that others do not. That is the nature of ordination, and for the NSM it will invariably mean feeling a powerful sense of isolation, not being safely one thing or the other, Church or world. It is not surprising that some NSMs want to abandon this particular boundary, but for the sake of the Kingdom of God, which matters much more than the Church, and only for which indeed the Church itself exists, it is to be hoped that they will not.

Their vocation and ministry is to be the symbol of God's working, an affirmation of the creativity of human beings being one with God's own purposeful activity. They are models for other Christians caught up in complexities and compromises they struggle to reconcile with their faith. They are there to affirm the work of those who struggle for justice and peace, wholeness and healing. They are there finally to be the priests of God's creation, bringing his world to him in prayer and worship, particularly in the offering of the Eucharist, as it awaits its final transformation:

'The created universe is waiting with eager expectation for God's sons to be revealed. It was made subject to frustration, not of its own choice but by the will of him who subjected it, yet with the hope that the universe itself is to be freed from the shackles of mortality and is to enter upon the glorious liberty of the children of God. Up to the present, as we know, the whole created universe in all its parts groans as if in the pangs of childbirth. What is more, we also, to whom the Spirit is given as the firstfruits of the harvest to come, are groaning inwardly while we look forward eagerly to our adoption, our liberation from mortality.'

(Rom. 8.19–23)

Perhaps most important of all, their ministry can help recall the whole Body of Christ to the ministry to which each of us is called: that of leaving behind that which is safe and secure, and going out to serve the Kingdom of God. It may mean we shall have to change our understanding of ministry, but whatever else such a ministry is, it most certainly is real.

CHAPTER FOUR

Between Men and Women

Churches are the sort of institutions which find change difficult. The joke that the Vatican likes to think in terms of centuries not years might be funny were it not for the sorts of mess the Roman Catholic Church has got itself into from time to time by being unable to adapt to change. The other churches, mainly by virtue of being smaller and younger, do not have precisely the same sort of fossilised structures which determine the response of Rome to new situations, but they nevertheless manifest many of the same symptoms. There are clear reasons why this should be so. A large voluntary society with a central core which has great power is bound to be conservative and fearful about change. This has nothing to do with theology – it is just a fact of organisational life, and one which can be amply illustrated.

The experience of Galileo is a classic example or, within the Church of England, the response to Darwin's *Origin of Species*. In so many instances there has been a manifest fear of and hostility towards those who have brought change. A second stage is a kind of truce in which some, generally far-sighted, individuals seek to find ways of encouraging people to recognise how groundless are their fears and that change can be incorporated without too much being at stake. Although some can never come to this point and remain permanently paralysed by fear or operate wholly in reaction to the new insights, before too long a third stage is reached in which the new insights become part of the received orthodoxy and their supporters are even hailed as prophets. An excellent example of this followed the publication in 1861 of *Essays and Reviews*, a collection of essays

by seven Oxford men which sought to find ways of incor-
porating modern learning into theology. The initial response of the Church at large was to seek to banish them
from their positions, and they were even dubbed the 'Seven
Against Christ'. A generation later their ideas had won
widespread acceptance and one of their number, Frederick
Temple, had become Archbishop of Canterbury. When one
considers the names and subsequent history of men such as
Hensley Henson, E. W. Barnes, John Robinson and David
Jenkins, the pattern of it has a depressingly familiar Anglican feel.

Even the technological and communication revolution,
which has taken place during the lifetime of so many of us,
the churches have been on the whole surprisingly slow to
grasp (though typically, having arrived so late, many in the
churches have now seemingly baptised modern technology
and would not think of any kind of communication without
the latest audio-visual aids!). At a banal level, the Church
Commissioners now provide interest-free loans for
stipendiary clergy to buy a motor car, these being regarded
as necessary for the performance of the job. Yet during
the 1930s a number of bishops made public statements
condemning the use of cars by clergy.

It is therefore perhaps not entirely surprising that the
churches have found it difficult to react and respond to the
sexual revolutions of this century: (a) the recognition of
how dominant sexuality is for a proper understanding of
what it means to be human; and (b) the demand by women
that their full humanity be recognised. The innate conservatism of the institution taken together with matters which are
in themselves uncomfortable for many people make this
particular revolution even harder to face than some others.

I am more than ever convinced that arguments presented
against the ordination of women to the priesthood, the
claims made by some that women are subordinate to men in
terms of headship or that they cannot 'image' the male
Christ, cannot be separated from the persistence of serious

sexual crime against women and their continued exploitation for male sexual gratification; nor is any of this unrelated to the sorts of relationship men have had with their mothers, something which figures so powerfully in the work of Sigmund Freud and the continuing work of psychoanalysis and psychotherapy. If we add to this the place of the Virgin Mary within the Christian tradition as the perfect woman (at one and the same time a mother and a virgin – every man's fantasy, and for women, a wholly inimitable model!) and the notion of 'Mother Church', it is not at all surprising that the matter cannot easily be dealt with.

Laws against sexual discrimination have now been in force for a good number of years in this country (though shamefully the churches have sought exemption for themselves from some of their dictates). As many women will confirm, the law is one thing – what cannot be changed are basic attitudes. These are formed in the earliest days of our being in the world, bonding with our mother and the subsequent experience of being mothered. Time and again psychotherapists return to these experiences as the basic shapers of our subsequent life, the foundations of the unconscious which continues to exercise so powerful an effect upon our later adult life.

The fact that many workplaces are full of photographs of bare-breasted women, that some daily newspapers include a 'page 3' girl, that most newsagents (not to mention specialist sex shops) have a shelf full of magazines featuring naked women, that men frequent striptease clubs and the like, are surely an adequate testimony to a certain confused sexuality in many men. Sexual assaults on women and children have a similar root.

Working in an institution where significant efforts have been made to eradicate sexist language I was recently reminded how different that is from what happens elsewhere listening to conversations in a sports club following a rugby match. I was simply amazed by the way in which women were spoken of and struck by the sheer weight of sexual language among a group of adults. If I didn't recognise how closely these views relate to the actual experience of some women on the receiving end of the (often unwanted) attentions of men I might simply have concluded that this bore out so much of Freud's understanding. As it is, I think the matter is more serious.

Women who recognise this inevitably have great difficulty in taking seriously the contentions of the opponents of the ordination of women to the priesthood that their reasons are primarily theological. When an all-male group in synod (as the House of Clergy was at the time) turns down equality for women, many women are not at all surprised, and they have a pretty shrewd idea what is really going on – and it has precious little to do with theology! For them it has much more in common with their experience of being abused, patronised and discriminated against in the workplace and the home. The Church may like to think of itself as a heavenly society – for many women it bears all the hallmarks of a typical earthly institution.

Whilst the debates about the ordination of women continue it is extremely difficult for the Church to claim that it is serious in its concern for the place of women in our society, though the way such debates are reported often does injury to the reality of ordained women in the Church. There have been ordained women clergy in the Church of England since 1987 (the Congregationalists led the way 68 years earlier). Before that there was an order of deaconesses which, although it required comparable training to that for the clergy, was in fact regarded officially as a lay order. In 1987 most of these deaconesses were ordained deacon and subsequently most women in training have been ordained deacon. That makes them full members of the House of Clergy, they may be called Reverend and can wear clerical dress. Some of them have been made Canons and one of my own colleagues, the Revd Stella Collins, in the autumn of 1989 was appointed as a Rural Dean in the diocese of Salisbury, the first woman non-stipendiary minister in the

Church of England to be so. So although as yet women cannot be ordained priest in the Church of England they can be ordained deacon, and in many places they are clearly recognised as fulfilling a representative ministry, representative of the Church and representative of God, something which has nothing at all to do with their gender and everything to do with the fact that they are received as they are simply by virtue of their ordination.

It is interesting to note how in recent years although there has been a clear falling off in the number of men being selected for training to the ordained ministry the comparable figure for women being selected has continued to rise, as has their number as a proportion of the whole:

Year	Men Recommended Stip.	NSM	Women Recommended Stip.		NSM	% Women of Total
1975	348	90	–	43	–	9.8
1976	254	102	–	55	–	15.4
1977	349	109	–	50	–	10.9
1978	376	126	–	44	–	8.7
1979	375	121	–	52	–	10.4
1980	404	121	–	73	–	13.9
1981	361	115	73	116	43	24.3
1982	350	110	60	105	45	22.8
1983	303	87	61	102	41	26.1
1984	306	92	68	117	49	29.3
1985	347	83	80	131	51	30.4
1986	363	84	87	136	49	30.4
1987	320	73	77	126	49	32.0
1988	252	50	80	131	51	43.3

(Figures published by ACCM)

Together with the large number of former deaconesses who were ordained deacon in 1987, the actual number of ordained women in the Church of England is now not inconsiderable. In terms of the non-stipendiary ministry the above figures are interesting in a number of ways. The first thing to notice is the steady fall in the number of men being

selected for the NSM from 1978 onwards, as well as the
proportion of selected women who opt for NSM:

| Year | NSM of Gender Group Recommended | |
	Men	Women
1981	24.1%	37.0%
1982	23.9%	42.8%
1983	22.3%	40.1%
1984	23.1%	41.8%
1985	19.3%	38.9%
1986	18.7%	36.0%
1987	18.5%	38.8%
1988	16.5%	38.9%

(ACCM Annual Statistics)

One other feature of recent ACCM statistics requires
notice: the proportion of women who train for either
stipendiary or non-stipendiary ministry via non-residential
training:

1984	1985	1986	1987	1988
53.8%	54.9%	45.8%	52.4%	54.3%

In terms of comparison with occupations outside the
employment of the Church these figures are not untypical in
that they point to the way in which more women than men
have to take part-time work. The Church in common with
the majority of 'secular' employers is thus becoming heavily
dependent upon a pool of low-paid or unpaid female
labour.

Yet as many women know only too well, the realities of
their life, in terms of children, home, and the expectations
both of their husband and society as a whole, militate
against this being any different. For a woman wanting to
work in the Church, the resistance to her non-acceptance of
the traditional role of wife and mother will be even greater.
It is fascinating to note that when the ASB Calendar was
being put together two of those to be commemorated were

Margaret, Queen of Scotland (who died in 1093) and
Josephine Butler (who died in 1907). As with others, the
Calendar lists the particular reason for which the Church
continues to pay them attention. Margaret of Scotland is
therefore described as 'Queen, Wife, Mother' and Josephine
Butler, 'Social Reformer, Wife, Mother'. No doubt those
responsible imagined they were saying something positive
and important about being a wife and a mother. But why are
none of the men, quite a few of whom were fathers and
husbands, not likewise defined (and much the same would
go for the category of virgin – again only ever used of female
virgins)? Surely this is because of a deep-rooted sexual
stereotyping which so characterises societies in which males
predominate, and which, ultimately, can easily imprison
women.

In a very real way therefore the strides that women have
made in the life of the Church are a mark of an advance,
albeit, when set in the continuing context of debates on the
ordination of women to the priesthood, limited. It is a
limited advance too because women in the churches share
with women working in secular contexts the constraints of
opportunity. Although there are times when a family will
change house and move to another part of the country
because of the woman's work, such are few, and much more
usually it is for the husband's job that such moves have to be
made. Equally when children are born there are some
households in which the father will not go out to work and
instead act as househusband, but they are few in number.
Almost always it is the woman who sets on one side the
possibilities of career advancement in favour of the family –
a pattern which much Church life up to the present time has
supported.

Thus even discounting the hostility engendered against
the ministry of women in the churches (though it is hard to
do so when one remembers how much there is and how
painful) women seeking ordination face all the same problems and difficulties with which other women have to

contend in the realm of secular employment. That would certainly account for the fact that even though things have begun to change, and numbers of women are going up all the time, there are still far fewer women coming forward for ordination than men (though if the 1988 figures for men above are repeated too often this may well change before too long). It would appear that being unattached and mobile is the chief requirement of candidates for the stipendiary ministry. Between 1984 (when figures on the marital status of ordinands first became available) and 1988 an average of 65 per cent of those preparing for stipendiary ministry were single, and because a number of married women prepare for stipendiary ministry on non-residential schemes (and often are part-time stipendiary), it is safe to assume that the number of women actually preparing residentially for full-time stipendiary ministry is remarkably small.

As regards the non-stipendiary ministry for women, an average of more than 70 per cent in the same period were married. In terms of age when selected for training, an average of 54.4 per cent of those women preparing for stipendiary ministry were under 35 years, whilst an average of 85.5 per cent of those preparing for NSM were over 35 years. Figures do not actually exist showing which women were in part-time occupations at the time of selection though in 1988 36 per cent of those preparing for NSM were economically non-active as housewives. Of the rest by far the majority were teachers or playschool leaders, of which it can probably be assumed a fair proportion were working part-time.

Drawing some of these figures together we can begin to see that if you are a woman experiencing some kind of sense that you are called to offer yourself for ordination the possibilities begin to recede with marriage, children and age. A single woman has freedom of choice with regard to training – if she later gets married and has children the options for the exercise of ministry will begin to diminish. A married woman, whose husband's job ties her to a particular locale has considerably less freedom with regard to the possibilities of stipendiary ministry, for she may not be able to move to a college at the other end of the country (the nearest may be entirely inappropriate – a married evangelical woman ordinand living in Wakefield, for example, would hardly see the nearby anglo-catholic college at Mirfield as ideal!). These constraints grow as children come, both in terms of freedom to do a full-time residential course of training, as well as having to move children from one school to another for a short period of time before they have to be moved again (something of which, in my experience, women are more aware than men). Thus non-residential training may be the only option for many women who would want to opt for a stipendiary ministry, and for many, many more (something clearly borne out by the figures above), non-residential training for non-stipendiary ministry is the only option for the exercise of any kind of ordained ministry.

There are two things to be said of this. The first is that once again we notice how like the secular world the Church is as an employer. Whatever theological claims the churches may like to make of their identity and being, sociologically they bear all the hallmarks of any human institution, and any ecclesiology which does not take adequate account of that has not yet begun to be realistic. There is a tendency in all theology to be romantic and never more so than in the theology of the Church itself. Speaking of ourselves as the Body of Christ (a deeply biblical metaphor which has been given prominence through its use in the ASB Rite A liturgy) may sound very good, but just what does it mean? There is perhaps a very deep need for a more holistic approach to theology which seeks, for example, to hold together the highest hopes of ecclesiology with the more realistic awareness of the doctrine of the fall. With the advent of more women theologians in our universities (two of the major English chairs – in Birmingham and Bristol,

and another in Cambridge are now held by women) this is
something which may perhaps even be realistically hoped
for.

The second is to see that no matter what weaknesses of
the churches as institutions have been revealed, the advent
of NSM has brought the possibility of ordained ministry to
many women for whom it would otherwise have been quite
inaccessible.

We are at a stage in our understanding of the particular
contribution that women make to ministry which is little
more than tentative. I notice that in an excellent book on the
place of women in the life of the Church *Mirror to the
Church* not a single contributor was actually an ordained
woman reflecting upon her experience. Equally, in a book
dealing explicitly with the experience of ministers in secular
employment (Fuller 1986) – by which time the courses had
been training a significant number of women, hardly any
account was taken of the experience of women *qua* women,
and little otherwise. Once again none of the contributors
was actually a woman NSM.

Despite the lack of published material it is nevertheless
possible to begin to hear some of the stories that women
ministers are telling of themselves and which speak of the
sorts of possibilities that are going to be open to women in
the immediate future (however the issue of the ordination of
women to the priesthood is resolved). Once again, what is
most characteristic of these stories is that these NSMs are
finding themselves on the boundary.

The first and, perhaps, most obvious boundary between
themselves and their male counterparts is the extent to
which they can speak to other women in a way that no man
can. We saw in chapter three how the NSM, because she is
in secular employment, can speak to the lay members of the
Church about their work and its pressures in a way that no
stipendiary minister can – simply because they too are doing
'it' and living with 'its' pressures. This is equally the case for
women ministers and lay women. In the book *Mirror to the*

Church Jane Williams has a chapter 'Mothers, Chaos and Prayer' which deals with the experience of so many young Christian women that their attempts to live out some kind of spiritual life is constantly frustrated by the very real demands of small children and the chaos that inevitably follows them around.

I certainly recall many occasions when my wife expressed deep envy of me as a parish priest because I had to be 'up front' and freed of the delightful but extraordinarily demanding handful that is our younger daughter. How often too was it ever so easy for me as a parish priest with the obligation of the daily office to say to use this as an excuse to get out of the house at uncomfortable moments? How easy too for married clergy to make sure, using this obligation, that their own spirituality continues to have space — but what then of the wife and mother at home?

Nor can we assume that such pressures diminish as children grow. Not only do older children bring other pressures but family life itself is often something which is managed by the wife and mother; she is the one who has the 'holding together' brief, and the task of reconciling this with the demands of faith in terms of finding space and time to do justice to which ever kind of response she wants to make to God simply for herself, is not easy at all.

The NSM knows all about these pressures from her own experience (indeed they probably became even worse once she began her training), for although many women wait until the children are old enough to afford her some more space, the demands of training are not inconsiderable, and as the one with the role of holding the family together, extra demands in the life of the family will very often fall upon her, and usually just when she was planning some time for study or (as happened to one student) minutes before she was due to leave home for a residential weekend. This is not to denigrate the support that many students receive from their husbands, simply to state what is more often than not a fact – that when crisis comes in the context of home and family it is almost always the wife and mother who has to hold together the rest as they deal with it. Because this happens so spontaneously in most families many men meet an awareness of it with a considerable degree of hostility and denial – and that too is part of the lot that many wives and mothers have to carry.

The NSM has her experience to offer other women – her own experience of struggling with God in the context of all the conflicts that make up life of so many other women. Some years ago I heard a clergyman, now somewhat eminent and a noted liturgical scholar, using his Sunday sermon to talk about the worshipping needs of the mothers of young children. In a way and to his credit, by focussing upon their plight, he was showing an awareness that not every man has (and certainly not in the 1960s when I heard this). But his advice, which was that mothers should regard the attention they gave to their children during the service as their worship left me, even then, uneasy. If the Church, and he in particular, gave so much attention to the reformation and formation of liturgy, why was it that the mothers of young children were to be denied their own full participation in it? If looking after children was worship, why bother coming to church and enduring considerable discomforts (pews are not easy places to entertain small children – nor some congregations the most appreciative of audiences of one's efforts!) when attending to them at home was much easier? Above all, one wondered upon what experience he was basing his words.

Of course any ordained woman who has been a mother can be of use to other women in this way, but as most NSMs are married, and have had children, and are possibly still having to deal with such things (that is why she is an NSM and not stipendiary), she is particularly well placed. This does not mean that it should be assumed of every woman NSM that of course she should be put to work only with women. Nevertheless the needs of lay women do need attention and many NSMs indeed discover important and particular ministries in this area.

A second element in which the woman NSM has something of vital importance to offer the whole Church concerns the extent to which as a woman she will most likely be involved in the day-to-day practicalities of home making – cooking and cleaning. She does not inhabit some kind of mysterious realm which it often seems to be assumed that many male clergy inhabit, but a very ordinary and matter-of-fact world, and it is within and out of that context that she ministers. One of the great classics of the spiritual life is Brother Lawrence's *The Practice of the Presence of God* which speaks of the monastic kitchen as the place where this particular monk discovers the path to contemplation. His discovery of God present among the pots and pans is often praise by spiritual writers, yet what is often overlooked is that the world of the pots and pans is predominantly that of women. That God can be met and encountered in the ordinary is something which the woman NSM has to offer simply because she spends so much of her time 'in the ordinary'. Why is it I wonder that whenever I think of George Herbert's poem 'The Elixir' it is always a woman I picture in the verse:

> 'A servant with this clause
> Makes drudgery divine;
> Who sweeps a room as for thy laws
> Makes that, and the action, fine?'

Closely related to the element of the woman NSM as the one who ministers out of the context of the most ordinary is the experience of many women ministers that their presence in the life of a local church can help to break down some of the barriers between clergy and lay, the pyramidal or hierarchical model which can characterise the life of many parishes. It is hard to see 'Mother' being used as 'Father' is and raises further questions about the latter in any case (though Jesus' own teaching on the matter has long been disregarded). Describing someone as 'Deacon Janet' sounds so peculiar that in most instances the first part is dropped and many deacons have discovered that they are primarily known just by their Christian name, even when the tradition of that particular congregation has been much more formal. The knock-on effect seems to be that the priest too in turn becomes known by his Christian name. In itself the issue is far less important than, though symbolic of, the issue of authority whereby clerical titles and the very position of cleric can easily isolate and protect the minister in a way quite contrary to the best hope for ministry as being about service.

A fourth element which belongs to the woman NSM (though perhaps to all ordained women who have had children) is the specifically sexual role of a woman in a liturgical context, in which she brings with her the past which the congregation has has known of her as being pregnant, giving birth and feeding a child. There is still considerable misapprehension among many men about these womanly processes intimately bound up with their own sexual experience and fear and these are closely allied with the issue of power (as Alyson Peberdy has shown in *Mirror to the Church*). I recall the amazement I experienced some years ago at the reaction of a senior clergyman to the presence of an extremely attractive woman who was appointed to serve at the Eucharist he was about to celebrate. Although on other occasions he had been perfectly happy for lay assistants to serve in their ordinary clothes, he was clearly so disturbed by her physical appearance and presence that he insisted she wear some kind of garb which presumably rendered her sexless. Given that many men find the sexuality of women both alluring and disturbing it may become a channel for some healing that women ministers *qua* women begin to fulfil a visible liturgical role. (It is such a pity that so much of this is unexpressed during debates on the ordination of women to the priesthood and that there is still a considerable degree of reticence among Christians in speaking about sexuality, even when it is clearly playing so major a part in the life of the Church).

This needs to be extended however beyond the boundaries of the church building. Women as representatives of God and the Church may well be extremely disturbing to men who can see them as creatures of which to be afraid and which they need to dominate or hurt. It is well known that some lay women have fantasies about male clergy and their sexuality, perhaps the presence of women clergy can begin to do some work of healing within men by bringing with themselves a God-image which is itself much more wholesome and capable of meeting the actual hurts which can so powerfully affect how men behave with regard to women.

Certainly in a workplace a woman NSM could dare to deal with the subject of sexuality in a direct way, perhaps in reference to an apparent small matter such as the ever-present nude on a calendar. Because most women NSMs, if they are in secular employment, do not find themselves in places where this aspect of male sexuality is so blatant (most are teachers or work in a health-related capacity) dare we hope that this is something which male NSMs also need to be dealing with in their places of work. Of course this may well be received as the 'prudishness of the vicar' but it need not provided it is addressed directly and honestly – something which rarely happens with regard to male sexuality. The NSM in a workplace really is a part of the place and as such has the right to raise these matters in a way that no industrial chaplain could (nor ever would, for a whole host of reasons largely to do with their own urgent desire to be liked).

Amazingly (as it now appears) my own ordination training managed to avoid the issues of sexuality save perhaps in one lecture on Freud. In an all-male environment we were not encouraged to look at our own sexuality, though a number of people recognised that the presence of a strong undercurrent of active homosexuality indicated that it was crying out for help. I suspect that this experience is fairly typical. Very few clergy seem able to handle sexuality at all well, and the growing incidence of clergy marital break-down (something which is beginning to cause all sorts of alarm bells to ring) suggests we may well be reaping the consequences of our former neglect.

The course for which I work at least attempts to encour-age students to do some work on their own sexual experi-ence, whether active in terms of actual relationships or passive in terms of their basic sexuality and all that it means. It is not easy of course and no one could, nor should, be forced to go beyond what they can manage. On the other hand students can be encouraged to recognise that by facing this aspect of themselves what they are doing is also a part of their spiritual quest, the discovery of how to serve the Kingdom of God with all that we are and with a profound awareness of where we ourselves are in need of healing. None of us can go out and minister without recognising our needs, and not for nothing is there a powerful tradition within the Church of the finest healers actually being the wounded healers.

It has taken the Church a very long time to realise just how much it had to gain from a treasure that was at one and the same time visible yet buried. Recent research has re-vealed that it was not always so and that in the early Church women had a much greater role than has sometimes been assumed. The heart of the problem has been the way in which many men (though many women have been, and still are, happy to collude) have preferred women to be primarily those who make the active life of men possible, have pushed onto them the motherly role of nurturing, and have not only done so in the full knowledge that for many women such a role is indeed their by nature, but have backed such a pattern up with a whole theology. It has of course served its purpose and for generations the Church has made full use of non-stipendiary women cleaners, menders, makers, bakers and even more, since the mid-sixteenth century, the office of the non-stipendiary clergy wife. This latter office has been of course one of the principal ways in which women have been able to contribute something very powerful of their own to the structures of ecclesiastical life. Writing in Salisbury and passing the Bishop's House each day on my way to work, how could I ever overlook Mrs Proudie and the enormous influence she had upon the diocese of Barchester? No doubt there were women such as her; far more likely have been generations of women whose pastoral and organisational skills have been in much demand by parishioners, and whose best energies have been spent in the service of God and the Church in such ways.

It is abundantly clear that non-stipendiary ministry is opening up for many women the possibility of a ministry to which they believe themselves called, to which they believe they can give themselves in the service of God. Of course it has to be negotiated around many practicalities and other competing demands. Often I am amazed at how some of our students manage their training given all these other press-ures – but they do. Given space by incumbents sensitive enough to recognise the boundaries with which women are working, it is also possible for them to develop strong and whole working relationship which give birth to a rich ministry.

It seems too that God often renews the Church from outside. It was so time and again with Israel. It was so long ago when a young woman encountered light and was filled with grace and became the God-bearer. It happened too very early on the first day of a particular week when one woman in particular was singled out and given the greatest commission ever entrusted to another human being. In this century too God has done the unpredictable. A movement which seemed to have little to do with Christianity has begun, slowly and very late, to bring about renewal and new opportunity. It is to be hoped that even now it is not too late for the Church to seize it, and that many more women can have the authority of God to find their own place on the boundary where he has set them.

CHAPTER FIVE

Between the Christian and the Human

Most parish clergy could testify to a constant sense of amazement that week by week and month by month people come knocking on their doors asking for the occasional offices. In 'post-Christian' Britain that is surprising. Apparently one in three children are still baptised and a high proportion of people continue to present themselves for the solemnization of holy matrimony. Of course the reasons that bring people are complex, and not every parent, and certainly not every couple seeking a church wedding, could actually say either that they believed in God or, if they did, that it made any difference to their lives whatsoever. Although opinion polls continue to find that as many as 80% of the population claim belief in God, there is little evidence to suggest that this makes much difference to the way they live, and very much fewer regard themselves as committed members of one of the churches.

There have long been arguments about what it means to be a Christian and whether or not being a Christian means being a member of one of the churches. There have always been those who wish to draw the lines of demarcation between Christian and non-Christian very firmly, and in so doing, have largely believed that they have been acting in accordance with God's own way of discriminating between people. Such a pattern of thinking takes a number of forms. There is the catholic notion that 'outside the Church there is no salvation', the Church defined by the boundaries of the baptised. At the other end of the theological spectrum lies the evangelical notion that baptism alone suffices nothing and that unless there is a living relationship with the risen Lord Jesus there can be no salvation. In both there are clearly defined groups of Christians and Rest, and the underlying supposition is that one lot are bound for heaven whilst the others are doomed to hell (or at least, in the Catholic tradition, something definitely less than heaven).

Between these two positions the Church of England as an established Church often finds itself caught in a complex compromise. Some clergy and congregations find this unbearable and prefer to operate much more like a sect in the way they seek to draw their boundaries. Others rejoice in the compromise and welcome the hesitant and half-committed who come asking for something without any real understanding of why and not over-concerned about it either. The writings of Wesley Carr suggest that these encounters bear enormous creative potential.

One of the features of the way in which clergy encounter those who do not have any, or a minimal, church involvement, is that they do so from a position of strength. It tends to be on their own territory and on matters in which the clergy have all the expertise and power. This means that people are never quite themselves. It also means that from the beginning of their involvement people tend to be, in some small way at least, sufficiently favourably disposed towards the Church that they have made the effort to come and knock on the door. As I know from experience this does not necessarily make the encounter easy for the ordained minister, but it does provide a considerable degree of protection for him or her.

NSMs too know and meet people in their work who are basically kindly disposed towards the Church, but their encounters differ from those of their parochial colleagues in two particular and distinct ways. The first is that they do not relate to them from a position of superiority or security: people can speak the truth to them without fear that they might be putting anything at risk. The second lies in the fact that although the parish clergy do indeed meet people of diverse views they rarely meet those who are violently opposed to them. Although they may still be asked to perform the funeral of someone who did not believe in God, they rarely meet with (in any real sense of the word, which is to say to 'get into genuine dialogue with') that two-thirds of the population who choose not to bring their children for baptism nor those who do not come for a church wedding. Equally very few come into contact with those whose religious beliefs are quite different and who increasingly make up a significant minority in British society. The NSM however does encounter such people every day, and how is she to respond? Is she there to proselytise, to win converts? Is she there to be a silent presence? How does she understand the difference between someone who is a Christian and someone who is not? And how is any of this to affect her dealings with people because of her status as an ordained minister?

These two issues, that of ministering from strength to weakness, and the second of ministry in the context of encounter with a non-Christian world both have their roots in the doctrine of the human person. What does it mean to be a human person and what is being assumed or required by Christian faith as a requirement for human beings to be acceptable to God?

In Romans 5, St Paul makes use of the story of Adam. Although the stories contained within Genesis are familiar to us, there is no evidence that they were to the majority of those writers whose works make up our Old Testament; indeed apart from a passing mention in 1 Chronicles 1.1 there is no mention of Adam other than in Genesis. This could mean one of two things, either they were unconcerned with these stories, or (and more likely) they largely did not know of them. From what we know it seems likely that the stories which make up the pre-history of humankind, contained in Genesis 1–11, were only prefixed to the stories of the Patriarchs after most of the rest of the Old Testament books had been completed. Thus it was only in that period we call 'inter-testamental' (approximately 150 BC–AD 50) that much interest was shown in these stories. Apocryphal and Apocalyptic writings from this period make much use of them and it seems not unlikely that these were known and used in rabbinic instruction at the time when St Paul studied under Gamaliel (Acts 22.3) and that his use of them reflects the knowledge derived from this source.

St Paul's use of the stories of Adam is limited to Romans 5 and 1 Corinthians 15 (there are brief references in 1 Timothy, but this is normally regarded as being a later work) and in any case the point he is seeking to make is more concerned with the place of Christ than developing theories about Adam. Certainly there is no 'doctrine of the Fall' present within St Paul, and in the years following it is worth noting that the extant writings of the early fathers show remarkably little interest in such things, though it is not wholly absent. This is not altogether surprising as there were many matters of a much more pressing nature with which to deal and especially at a time when the realities of martyrdom hung over the Church for long periods. Theological speculation awaited a period of tranquillity, when more urgent matters, such as those expressed by and embodied in the creeds, had already been settled. Of course the reality of sin was taken seriously throughout this period. The overcoming of sin was after all the purpose of the incarnation and death of Christ. Those who belonged to the Church knew full well that by baptism they had entered into a new creation and that sin no longer held them captive. That is not the same however as a fully-developed doctrine of sin, which had to wait for the coming of St Augustine of Hippo, in North Africa.

Augustine was brought to the expression of his views largely through engagement in controversy. Until this time he had broached the subject of the sinful nature of human beings in much the same way as other Patristic writers before him had, which is to say, he took it for granted without attempting to be over-specific. Nor indeed did he deal with the subject in any explicit way even in his Confessions, though it was a phrase within them which led to his arguments.

The person with whom Augustine was to enter into dispute was Pelagius, a British monk, possibly of Irish origin. He arrived in Rome in AD 400 and was deeply shocked by what he regarded as the low state of moral conduct there. Feeling that greater moral effort was required he was then dismayed by a section from Augustine's Confessions:

> 'I have no hope at all but in thy great mercy. Grant what thou commandest and command that thou wilt. Thou dost enjoin upon us continence, "And when I knew", saith one, "that none could be continent, except God gave it" (Wisdom 8.21), this was also a part of wisdom, to know whose gift it was.'

> (Confessions Bk. 10.40)

Pelagius believed that it was precisely such teaching that ultimately led to the sort of apparent moral unconcern he witnessed in Rome, but that, perhaps even more importantly, it bore witness to what he believed was an unacceptable doctrine of God:

> 'We ascribe to the God of knowledge the guilt of twofold ignorance; ignorance of his own creation and of his own commands. As if, forgetting the weakness of man, his own creation, he had laid upon men commands which they were unable to bear. And at the same time (God forgive us!) we ascribe to the Just one unrighteousness and cruelty; the first by complaining that he has commanded the impossible, the second, by imagining that a man will be condemned by him for what he could not help; so that (the blasphemy of it!) God is thought of as seeking our punishment rather than our salvation ... God has not willed to command anything impossible, for he is righteous; and he will not condemn a man for what he could not help, for he is holy'.

> (Letter to Demetriadem 16)

To Pelagius it seemed that St Augustine was suggesting that without the grace of God we are eternally doomed simply by virtue of the nature we possess which, having been made this way, cannot fulfil what God requires. He found such an idea absolutely abhorrent:

> 'Everything good and everything evil, in respect of which we be either worthy of praise or blame, is done by us, not born with us'

> (De peccato originali 14)

A major part of Augustine's thinking on these matters related to the practice of infant baptism. This had been the widespread policy of the Church at least from the late second century and as it was acknowledged that the effect of baptism was to deliver and heal the person from their state of sin, the practice of infant baptism meant that babies must have inherited their sin. From this it was relatively straight-forward discovering within the stories of Adam the roots of that hereditary sin, and to which St Paul seemed so clearly to be referring in Romans 5.12: 'Therefore as sin came into the world through one man and death through sin, and so death spread to all men because all men sinned'. (It ought to be noted that in St Augustine's Latin text of this verse he read: 'so death passed to all men *in whom* [i.e. Adam] all sinned' rather than the Greek which reads '*in as much as* all men sinned – thus increasing the force of his argument).

Augustine saw the stories about Adam as straightforward history positing a time when Adam and Eve lived a truly free existence with wills naturally inclined towards righteous-ness with the grace of perseverance in that righteousness throughout their lives. Their freedom was from what St Augustine called 'concupiscence'. He derived this word again from his Latin Bible which used it to translate 'covet-ousness' in Romans 7.7. In Augustine's mind this word had definite and deep sexual associations. In consequence there developed a close relationship in his thinking between the corrupt nature of fallen humans and the sexual act, so that in positing the state of Adam and Eve before the fall he regarded them as wholly free from sexual passion. They were also immune to disease and death, and in due course would presumably have continued to enjoy their immortality in heaven.

Then came the catastrophe of their disobedience whereby they became captives of the devil through the mediation of a snake inspired by a fallen angel (though his identification, familiar to us through Christian doctrine, is nowhere present in the original text). This first sin changed the nature of Adam and Eve. Not only were they thereby bound to the consequences of their actions, but through procreation were bound to transmit them to the rest of humankind.

These consequences were the loss of immortality, the capacity to experience pain and passion, guilt (and the consequent liability to punishment), and the loss of free will with regard to sin (meaning that although we retain freedom in some respects what is lost is the freedom to do good). It is from here that St Augustine was able to develop his understanding of grace, whereby the Holy Spirit works within us that which is good.

Augustine was not suggesting that each person repeats the sin of Adam, something which Pelagius might have been willing to accept, but that each person has inherited the sin and guilt of Adam (much as in our own time an unborn child might well come to inherit the consequences of a mother's being infected with the AIDS virus). St Augustine described the human race as a *massa damnata*. This is a metaphor taken from the bakery. It refers to a batch of dough (massa) about to be made into bread. However it is discovered that it has been mixed with dirty water. It is now condemned (damnata) and rightly thrown out. Augustine then goes on to speak, because he sees it as much more important, of the redemption brought by Christ, the salvation which is brought about purely and simply by the grace of God.

It is abundantly clear that major issues were at stake in the dispute between Pelagius and Augustine, and that both seemed to be saying important things. The Council of Carthage in 417 condemned Pelagius, although not without some reservations, and it was not until the Council of Orange in 529 that this condemnation was fully recognised and Augustine's teachings endorsed. These teachings were to be highly influential in giving shape and form to medieval theological speculation in relation to the doctrines of the atonement and redemption. One of those most influenced by Augustine, and in his own turn highly influential, was Calvin who wrote:

'Therefore original sin is seen to be an hereditary depravity and corruption of our nature, diffused into all parts of the soul . . . wherefore those who have defined original sin as the lack of original righteousness with which we should have been endowed, no doubt include, by implication, the whole fact of the matter, but they have not fully expressed the positive energy of this sin. For our nature is not merely bereft of good, but is so productive of every kind of evil that it cannot be inactive. Those who have called it concupiscence have used a word by no means wide of the mark, if it were added (and this is what many do not concede) that whatever is in man, from intellect to will, from the soul to the flesh, is all defiled and crammed with concupiscence; or, to sum it up briefly, that the whole man is in himself nothing but concupiscence . . .'

(Institutes Vol. 2.31)

By the route of Calvin at the time of the Reformation this teaching finds clear expression in the *Book of Common Prayer*. A classic example of this is found in the collect for the Ninth *Sunday* after Trinity:

'Grant to us, Lord, we beseech thee, the spirit to think and to do always such things as be rightful; that we, *who cannot do any thing that is good without thee*, may by thee be enabled to live according to thy will; through Jesus Christ our Lord.'

An equally powerful expression of the essential depravity of the human condition can be found in the collects for Easter Day, Trinity 15, 16 and 19. Not surprisingly it is also a significant feature of the Articles of religion. Number 9, dealing with original sin states:

'Original Sin standeth not in the following of Adam (as the Pelagians do vainly talk;) but it is the fault and corruption of the Nature of every man, that naturally is engendered of the offspring of Adam; whereby man is very far gone from original righteousness, and is of his own nature inclined to evil, so that the flesh lusteth always contrary to the spirit; and therefore in every person born into this world, it deserveth God's wrath and damnation . . .'

Pelagianism has often been labelled the 'English heresy' on the grounds that the English seem somehow predisposed to a theology of self-reliance (no matter what the BCP may have said!). Others too have wondered whether Pelagius should have been wholly condemned and that perhaps some synthesis of he and St Augustine might have had more wholesome consequences for subsequent generations.

The binding of guilt to sexuality cannot be gainsaid nor the serious damage done to many denied. Equally a charge can be made that it has, through Calvin in particular, encouraged a lack of concern in Christians for those about them, whereby the saved become wrapped up in their own salvation and the piety consequent upon it, a sanctified fatalism and apathy. It can easily lead to the idea that those not baptised lie wholly and utterly beyond the concern of God so that proselytising becomes the only legitimate response to their plight. However there are some major reasons why Christians may be able to see that there is an alternative to such an approach, and not least among them are some serious flaws in the way in which this theology of the human person has been arrived at and perpetuated.

In the first place there is the question of history. St Augustine's theory depends upon the literal truth of the stories of Adam and Eve. Once we no longer accept such a view of their historicity and recognise their mythological nature, we are presumably no longer bound to hold the doctrines dependent upon them. Indeed as we advance we shall discover that for other reasons it can be theologically advantageous for us to recognise that those stories of Genesis

1–11 are *not* literally true. Primarily this is so in relation to a consideration of the work of Christ, for if the end of His work has been redemption and restoration, a literal account of Genesis seems to assume either or both of the following:

(a) – that God's omniscience did not foresee the 'fall' and the consequence that God must be less that omniscient or wicked in pretending that what was to happen was not going to;

(b) – that had there not been such a 'fall' which required Christ's coming to correct, human beings would never have known either the reality of the Trinity (which after all was only revealed in the incarnation) or the sort of love revealed by the Incarnation. This latter paradoxical problem finds delightful expression in a number of places, notably the Exsultet or Easter Proclamation sung in the Easter Vigil (interestingly these verses are omitted from the Anglican version included in *Lent, Holy Week and Easter*) and the medieval hymn *Adam Lay Y-bounden*:

> 'This is the night when Jesus Christ
> broke the chains of death
> and rose triumphant from the grave.
> What good would life have been to us,
> had Christ not come as our redeemer?
> Father, how wonderful your love for us!
> How boundless your merciful love!
> To ranson a slave
> you gave away your Son.
> *O happy fault, O necessary sin of Adam,*
> which gained for us so great a redeemer'

> 'Adam lay y-bounden
>   Bounden in a bond;
> Four thousand winters
>   Thought he not too long;
> And all was for an apple,
>   An apple that he took,
> As clerkes finden written
>   In theire book.

Ne had the apple taken been,
   The apple taken been,
Ne hadde never our Lady
   A been heaven's queen.
Blessed be the time
   That apple taken was!
Therefore we may singen
   "Deo gracias"'.

In the later middle ages a number of theologians, notably Duns Scotus and St Bonaventure, recognised this problem and suggested that the incarnation would have happened anyway, but it is difficult to avoid the feeling that their arguments are unnecessary and that a simpler solution to their problem could be found simply by freeing themselves of the need to see Adam as a historical figure.

Related to this is the old joke told of Adam, 'Did he fall or was he pushed?' It bears witness to the recognition that before the fall Adam might well have been free and immortal, but that only by coming to terms with evil through his experience of it would he be capable of any kind of moral growth. Hence no fall, no growth. (In this respect we can perhaps see the value to our moral and spiritual growth of temptation, someting positively recognised in the stories of the temptation of Jesus, whereby Jesus is only brought to a deeper understanding of his work because he has had to come to terms with the alternatives). If we bind ourselves to a literal account of the fall we bind ourselves to seeing God as less than loving because devious in wanting men and women to be capable of less than he has actually made them. Equally it would mean that in unregenerated (i.e. unbaptised) people no possibility for good exists something plainly contrary to simple observation and no amount of theological convolution can make it otherwise.

These are real problems even though we can see how and why Augustine has led us towards them. He knew from his own experience, as did Paul before him (c.f. Romans 7.13–25), that there was a struggle within himself, a struggle both moral and spiritual, and which he identified with his nature, something inherited simply by virtue of having been born human, being at war with the sanctifying work of grace within him. He knew too the work and reality of Christ as having brought about the reconciliation of himself as a sinner with God, indeed we might say that it is the overwhelming nature of this conviction that motivates Augustine and which led him into his dispute with Pelagius. The emphasis he places upon sinful nature we might think over-pessimistic but he undoubtedly prepares us for seeing human beings as they can be at their worst. The vicissitudes of twentieth century evil, the continuing experience within many people of a sense of alienation and isolation or overwhelming guilt are realities which reflect the sort of human nature which Augustine recognised within himself, a nature which needs God but which is naturally separated from God. If we experience anxiety about his statement of original sin, about its dependence upon a literal fall, if we feel he has exaggerated the gulf between ourselves and God, and recognise that his views have often caused great harm in many people's lives, we ought also to be clear that we may indeed free ourselves from the particular form of his statements about nature and original sin, but we do need to be able to continue to take as seriously as he that separation from God, both for persons and societies, the terrible consequences of which have been and are only too apparent in human experience.

The influence of Augustine and his views on original sin has been extensive and at times has tended to obscure the fact that alternatives have existed within the Christian tradition which, whilst still taking sin seriously, say something different about human nature. One of these also makes use of material from Genesis:

'Then God said, "Let us make human beings in our image, after our likeness, to have dominion over the fish in the sea, the birds of the air, the cattle, all wild animals on land, and everything that creeps on earth". God created human beings in his own image; in the image of God he created them; male and female he created them.'

(Genesis 1.26f)

'This is the list of Adam's descendants. On the day when God created human beings he made them in his own likeness. He created them male and female, and on the day when he created them, he blessed them and called the man.'

(Genesis 5.1f)

'because in the image of God has God made human beings.'

(Genesis 9.6)

There has been disagreement among Old Testament commentators as to whether or not such language was intended to refer to some kind of physical resemblance to God, i.e. that God is somehow human-shaped. On the whole two things militate against this view. The first is that the creation story shows a radical re-working of an original Babylonian myth which was much more anthropomorphic suggesting that the writers were precisely *not* wanting to say such a thing. The second is that there is such a strong element in the Jewish tradition against idolatry (c.f. Exodus 20.4) that to include the suggestion that God was in human-form would be to tend towards the possibility of images (and it is worth noting in this respect that debates on this subject during the Iconoclastic crisis in the eighth century, in which the views of St John of Damascus triumphed at the Seventh Ecumenical Council in 787 which allowed the painting of images and icons *because* after the Incarnation it was recognised that God had been made visible in human form).

It seems likely that in speaking of human beings 'in the image and likeness of God' the Genesis tradition is referring to mankind as the crowning glory of creation as ruler and lord (though such languge is now somewhat unfashionable). Echoing the thought of Genesis 1, the psalmist notes:

'When I look up at your heavens, the work of your fingers,
at the moon and the stars you have set in place,
what is a frail mortal that you should be mindful of him,
a human being, that you should take notice of him?

Yet you have made him a little less than a god,
crowning his head with glory and honour.
You make him master over all that you have made,
putting everything in subjection under his feet:
all sheep and oxen, all the wild beasts,
the birds in the air, the fish in the sea,
and everything that moves along ocean paths.'

(Psalm 8, 3–8)

Within Christian thinking there have been two ways of thinking about being made 'in the image and likeness of God', the first, what we might call the direct, the second, the mediated.

An example within Christian writings of the direct use of the theme can be found in 1 Cor. 11.7 or James 3.9 where both writers use it without any attempt at clarification as to meaning, and in the former passage Paul is clearly using it to refer to males, something which the Genesis text explicitly denies.

Later theologians were less reticent in their interpretation of the theme even if there was not total agreement either among them or even within them. For example, Clement of Alexandria in one work applies the phrase to man's intellect, whilst in another to the human capacity for reproduction and creativity. Gregory of Nyssa in one place sees intellect and free will as the essential characteristics of the divine image, and in another applies it to the host of spiritual gifts with which God has enriched mankind. The fourth century writer Epiphanius of Cyprus reflects upon the number of possible alternatives thus:

'There is no need at all to define or affirm in what part of us that which is the divine image is effectuated, but we should simply confess that the image is in man, so that we do not reject God's grace and refuse to believe in Him. For whatever God says is true, even if it escapes our understanding in some respects'.

(Against Heresies 70.2)

As time advanced however it was the intellect, the faculty of reason, that which so obviously separates man from the animals, which predominated in theological thought as the seat of the divine image. The Hellenistic influence upon such thinking is clear where the 'intellectual principle' was regarded as the highest form of human life, truly the mark of the divine origins of the human soul. Hebrew thought did not divide humans up so easily into body, soul and spirit, but once such divisions underlay Christian anthropology, it was not wholly surprising that such an emphasis began to be placed upon the intellect as characteristic of mankind. The impact of Aristotelian thought upon St Thomas Aquinas for example, has meant that such thinking has predominated within the Western tradition although Calvin departed from this in thinking of the image and likeness as reflected in the relationship between man and God, in which he has been followed by Barth who placed emphasis upon the capacity within mankind for covenant with God (Barth resists the idea that the image and likeness is anything less than a social characteristic, i.e. it is not something possessed by individuals).

Modern thought has tended to prefer the concept of relationship and been somewhat dismissive about what has sometimes been seen as the élitist concept of the intellect. Certainly in Greek philosophy there was an emphasis upon the intellect as morally higher than other human activities, and thus upon the philosophers as the highest of all (in which the writings of e.g. the fifth century Denys the Areopagite, have tended to equate with contemplation in the Christian tradition). However this should not mean that there is not something of value herein. There is no actual need to link 'intellect' with 'intellectual' in its corrupt and pejorative sense as referring to a small élite of academics. The intellect, in the sense of the reasoning factor in human beings, remains the foundation of the possibility of moral- ity, and without the concept of morality human beings are most certainly not differentiated from the animals. If it has been lost sight of in recent writing this may in part be accounted for by its link with the idea of the soul or mind which has become unfashionable in philosophical circles.

The second approach is what we can call the mediated and refers to seeing the 'image and likeness' as it were through a particular prism provided by Christology. The roots of this are to be found in St Paul:

> 'He [Christ] is the image of the invisible God; his is the primacy over all creation. In him everything in heaven and on earth was created, not only things visible but also the invisible orders of thrones . . .'

(Col. 1.15f)

> '. . . the glory of Christ, who is the image of God'

(2 Cor. 4.4)

To these can be added:

> '. . . in this the final age he has spoken to us in his Son, whom he has appointed heir of all things; and through him he created the universe. He is the radiance of God's glory, the stamp of God's very being.'

(Hebrews 1.2f)

> '. . . to see me, is to see him who has sent me.'

(John 12.45)

> 'Anyone who has seen me has seen the Father.'

(John 14.9)

There is here the beginnings of a change of mode in thinking about creation, a movement towards what in theology is known as soteriology (the understanding of salvation) and eschatology (the understanding of the end [or purpose] of all things). It maintains that we can only understand the meaning of the Genesis affirmations in the light of the revelation of God in and through Christ, that the image and likeness in which we are made is the image and likeness of Christ. It is as if he is the archetype, and that if we are to understand what is to be understood as human nature it is to him we have to look and not merely the substance of which the copies are formed. A contemporary Greek theologian Panayiotis Nellas describes it thus:

> '. . . the ontological truth of man does not lie in himself conceived as an autonomous being – in his natural character-istics, as materialist theories maintain; in the soul or intellect, the higher part of the soul, as many ancient philosophers believed; or exclusively in the person of man, as contempor-ary philosophical systems centred on the person accept. No: it lies in the Archetype. Since man is an image, his real *being* is not defined by the created element with which the image is constructed, in spite of the iconic character which created 'matter' itself possesses, but his uncreated Archetype.'

(Deification in Christ p. 33)

This means of course that there is an essentially dynamic quality about our understanding of human beings, in so far as we can only come to think of ourselves in terms of becoming, what we shall be:

> 'And because for us there is no veil over the face, we all see as in a mirror the glory of the Lord, and we are being transformed into his likeness with ever-increasing glory . . .'

(2 Cor. 3.18)

> '. . . until we all attain to the unity inherent in our faith and in our knowledge of the Son of God – to mature manhood, measured by nothing less than the full stature of Christ.'

(Ephesians 4.13)

Related to this essentially Christological perspective on the image and likeness is a Trinitarian emphasis, that being made in the image and likeness of God, it is in the image and likeness of God as Trinity, which is to say a community of persons not a divine solitary. To writers such as Kenneth Leech the Patristic emphasis upon this is not merely of interest but essential to the possibilities of a genuine social theology:

> 'The doctrine of the Trinity is an assertion that within the Godhead itself there is society and equality of relationship and humanity is called to share in that divine life. Against the Arian heretics, the church insisted that God could and did share his nature with man, that we might be "sharers in the divine nature" (2 Peter 1.4). The Arian god, on the other hand, was lonely, remote and uninvolved, and did not share his nature with man because he could not. His relationship with man was that of a tyrant to his slaves, and St Athanasius drew a connection between this theology of the Arians and their oppression of the poor.'

> (The Social God p. 7)

In other words, if we are to understand human nature aright as made in the image and likeness of the Trinity, it is as persons not individuals, and persons in relationship that essentially characterises our being, albeit a being which is dynamic and known properly only in terms of what it is to be, or as what it will be in terms of Christ, the true person.

There can be no doubt that Augustine was clear that Adam and Eve were made in the image and likeness of God but his understanding of original sin is such that he believed that in subsequent humanity this image was worn out and defaced, using the imagery of a coin stamped with the image of the head of state. Luther was to go even further professing that the image of God was totally lost through sin. It is however possible to have a view of sin, which whilst taking it seriously, does not need to take so pessimistic a view.

In this understanding sin is seen as the state of our being which means we constantly fall short of what might be, the failure to realise our human potential as persons in relationship with God and, consequently, with one another. One of the most important of contemporary Greek lay theologians, Christos Yannaras, describes it thus:

'Sin is not a nature, an evil nature which exists hypostatically as the opposite pole to the divine existence and life of love. There is nothing in God's creation which is hypostatically and naturally evil, not even the devil himself. Sin is failure, a failure as to existence and life: it is the failure of persons to realize their existential "end", to confirm and conserve the uniqueness of their hypostasis through love.

This failure on the part of persons is bound to have consequences for the nature of man, since it distorts the nature and fragments it, transferring its existential possibilities from the freedom and distinctiveness of the person to the instinctive and absolute need for survival of the individual'.

(The Freedom of Morality p. 34)

Falling short of all that could be, the human person is left seeking self-preservation and self-perpetuation, the basic sin of pride present in individuals and nations. In the post-Freudian and post-Christian age indeed, wriggling to free ourselves from the residue of guilt inherited from the Western obsession with sin as transgression, there have been those who have argued that self-preservation and self-perpetuation in the form of will-to-power are a legitimate life-style in an essentially corrupt world in which 'good' and 'evil' are descriptions of no more than relativities. Such an individual justification is not unlike those who in the churches have striven for an essentially individual atonement. Both alike are failures in repentance, which means a change in existential stance and not merely in behaviour. As St Paul wrote:

'Conform no longer to the pattern of this present world, but be transformed by the renewal of your minds.'

(Rom. 12.2)

Paul is here saying that it is not enough simply to change the content of our thinking, perhaps by being more religious, it is to realise that the very shape of our thinking needs to be re-made in terms of a new relationship of trust in God, which is something quite different from simply being more religious. It looks forward in hope to the possibility of what is yet to be. St Irenaeus gave expression to this:

> 'God could have endowed man with perfection from the beginning, but man was as yet unable to receive it, for he was an infant. For the same reason, when our Lord came to us in these last days, recapitulating all things in himself, he came not as he could have done but in accordance with our ability to see him. He was certainly able to come to us in his incorruptible glory, but we would never have been able to endure its intensity'.
>
> (Against the Heresies 4.38)

We have been made for something, but are incapable, in our created nature of realising it; we have been made incomplete and await the completion and fulfilment for which we are made. (In this respect some theologians have differentiated between 'image' and 'likeness'; Prof. Georgios Mantzaridis, for example, notes that in the Septuagint the word 'likeness' expresses something dynamic yet not realised, whereas 'image' is something static but which in the context of Genesis 1 could be held to be a starting point for the attainment of the 'likeness'). It recalls the injunction of Jesus from the Sermon on the Mount:

> 'There must be no limit to your goodness, as your heavenly Father's goodness knows no bounds.'
>
> (Matthew 5.48)

in which the Greek word used is *teleioi*, from the root *telos* meaning 'end', and thus literally translated would be 'You must come to your true end as your heavenly Father is the true end' – a dynamic response to life which asks above all what we are made *for* rather than how we can escape *from* something. Rather than an obsession with transgressions and existential despair (a principle motivation in much of the Western religious tradition e.g. Luther, John Bunyan, John Wesley etc. and which continues to be used as a means of manipulation in some preaching) there is a recognition of the limitations of being finite and incomplete. No better expression of this can be found than in Augustine:

> 'O Lord thou hast made us for thyself, and we are thine, and our hearts are restless until they rest in thee'.
>
> (Confessions 1.1a)

though the inherent dangers of Augustine's subsequent line of argument need also the vital balance provided by Irenaeus of Lyons who, in the second century, gave expression to the most powerful statement of Christian humanism when he wrote:

> 'The glory of God is a man fully alive'.

In terms of the consequences of all this theology for the practice of ministry it is necessary to see the ways in which human beings have an existence and an identity and a value which they retain whether or not they ever come into such a position whereby the profession of faith is open to them. Those who, for example, speak of the women's movement in the Church as a sign of the way in which the Church has 'gone the way of the world' are failing to recognise that human beings made in the image and likeness of God are actually capable of doing things which are good and right, and that good things can emerge outside the Church, just as once Isaiah saw King Cyrus as the Lord's anointed. The advances in medicine for example have been genuine advances (as even the most ardent missionary who comes to his doctor for inoculation against tropical diseases before setting out to convert the heathen knows) even though many of the pioneers of such medical advance have been largely indifferent to the claims of the Christian faith. Again I recall a talented young musician who came to see me in something of a state. He had a passion for the music of Beethoven but was devastated to discover that his hero had no interest or concern whatsoever with Christianity. What,

I was left wondering, was the 'Christian music' for which my friend was searching? Perhaps it would be characterised by precisely the same absence of quality characteristic of the efforts of the so-called 'Christian novels' now being produced by some evangelical publishing houses.

Put another way I am suggesting that the doctrine of total depravity expressed in the collect for the Ninth Sunday after Trinity be utterly and completely rejected. Human beings are capable of a great deal and Christians do not have a monopoly of virtue. What then is the gospel for human strength? What have we to say to those who lead the way in terms of their commitment to human justice and truth, to those who recognise and rejoice in human achievement (notwithstanding a realism which recognises the limitations of such achievement) and who in so many ways are fully alive and yet neither know nor are too bothered about knowing God?

Traditionally Christians have approached people who seem strong with a deliberate attempt at discovering their Achilles' heels. Guilt, sickness and the ever-present fact of mortality are the customary modes of advance. Advances in the medical and human sciences have limited the first two; consequently the fact of death remains the most potent. It has always been so and much of the life of the medieval Church was characterised by the fear of post-mortem existence. No one of course will deny that death is a reality that awaits and confronts all people, and whilst it is one that many of us prefer not to spend too much time staring at, is it really necessary or actually compatible with the gospel that Christians should seek to manipulate people with it? Is fear any kind of worthy motive for coming to God? That surely can only lead to our despising God, for ultimately we hate that which we fear. If 'perfect love casts out fear' how can God possibly approve of fear being used to manipulate people into an awareness of his so-called love?

This tendency of Christians was noted from his prison cell by Bonhoeffer. Writing on 8 June 1944, he commented:

'The displacement of God from the world, and from the public part of human life, led to the attempt to keep his place secure at least in the sphere of the "personal", the "inner", and the "private". And as every man still has a private sphere somewhere, that is where he was thought to be most vulnerable . . .

. . . there is a kind of evil satisfaction in knowing that everyone has his failings and weak spots . . .

There is also a parallel isolation among the clergy, in what one might call the "clerical" sniffing-around-after-people's sins in order to catch them out . . .

Regarded theologically, the error is twofold. First it is though that a man can be addressed as a sinner only after his weaknesses and meannesses have been spied out. Secondly, it is though that a man's essential nature consists of his inmost and most intimate background; that is defined as his "inner life", and it is precisely in those secret human places that God is to have his domain!'

(Letters pp. 344f)

His observations remain pretty accurate though perhaps he doesn't quite do justice to the motives of some Christians. They too have to face the reality of death and I have sometimes wondered whether it is primarily their own anxieties about it that lead some to use the fact of death as an evangelistic tool against others. Some years ago I heard a recording of an evangelistic address by David Watson on the subject of death called 'Three Score Years and Then?'. He spoke on that occasion of his own certainty and confidence about death – indeed in one part even echoing Paul's words about longing to go and be with the Lord. His words stand in marked contrast to much of the account of his own dying a couple of years later. His last book *Fear No Evil* is moving, not least for being characterised, more than anything else, by an honesty about fear wholly absent in the earlier address.

Frankly, if we have nothing better to offer the world than the fear of death, then indeed we are impoverished, and it is abundantly clear that many people outside the Church know that. Seeing religion as a crutch for what they believe to be a crippled humanity, and one which they do not themselves need, they may well perhaps be over-stating their own self-reliance but it is often based upon a well-founded sense that what Christians often do is to make cripples of people who need not be, and that far from being fully alive, they are often perceived as life-denying and obsessed with the foibles and weaknesses of others. It is almost too obvious to need to state it, but many people have discovered a far greater degree of acceptance at times of crisis from those outside the churches than ever they have received from those within.

There are of course many people in need, but there are many with no obvious needs, some of whom could teach Christians a thing or two about life and its demands. One of the roles of the non-stipendiary minister is that of being the public face of the Church as it affirms human beings for themselves. We too easily lose sight of the fact that 'God so loved the world' that he sent his only Son – not because he hated it, and that his coming was to 'bring life, and life in all its fullness' (John 10.10).

Hence Bonhoeffer was led to conclude the theological observations of his above-mentioned letter:

> 'I therefore want to start from the premise that God shouldn't be smuggled into some last secret place, but that we should frankly recognise that the world, and people, have come of age, that we shouldn't run man down in his worldliness, but confront him with God at his strongest point . . .'

One of the many advantages in being an established church is the way in which on various occasions we are able to be affirmative of various and differing aspects of human achievement and effort which have nothing directly to do with the Christian religion as such. Although some clergy find such things difficult and other Christians may express anxiety at what looks like the Church being wheeled on to provide a modicum of respectability for the state and the *status quo*, nevertheless the presence of the Church in this way does at least point to the presence of God in human affairs and gives the lie to the view that he is only interested in the domain of religion. There might indeed be a place for anxiety if the role was limited to appearance, but the opportunity provided by such occasions need not be wasted. It is possible to speak to human strength of the demands of the Word of God for justice and truth in the public realm and not merely the limited world of private morality. It is possible to speak a word about stewardship and integrity; not a word of condemnation (which is ever so easy) but one which looks positively at the opportunities, though of course it needs to be supplemented by hard study of just what those possibilities are. Prophecy is not just about issuing demands and then fleeing into the security of the temple. Like Jeremiah it presupposes a willingness to stay with people and see the vision through, one way or the other.

The NSM in her work, in her sharing in the life of the local community, in her role in the family, in her role in the political life of nation and society has the opportunity for herself, and as a role model for other Christians, to be affirmative of the human condition and those people who give themselves in service, in one way or another, to their fellow human beings. And if things are going well, and people feel strong, then this is the time to acknowledge and recognise this, not to be hanging about in the hope that suddenly it might all go wrong so that we discover a place for God and ourselves.

Christians are called to be more human, not less. An actor friend, himself a priest, once wrote in a play: 'The trouble with some people is that they have learned to be religious before they have learned to be human' and it is unquestionably true of a good many Christians. For this reason it is incumbent upon NSMs in particular, though all Christians of course, that they seek to discover ways in which they can make a yet greater contribution to furthering the cause of being human through political involvement. This can only mean involvement in the processes of party politics, because in reality there is no other kind. That means taking sides and recognising that in working towards greater humanity it will not be possible to be on everyone's side and liked by all. Many parochial clergy recognise in this a genuine problem, something which clashes with their own perceived need to be the person holding things together in a community. That may or may not be so, though I would not underestimate the potential for extreme difficulty that a parish minister might well encounter once he or she begins to take party politics seriously. Whether or not a minister can opt for this must be something each one must wrestle with, but the NSM is not similarly constrained.

The Church is so programmed into ministering from strength to weakness that it will not be an easy shift of mode to begin recognising that many people really do not feel any apparent need for religion and, even more, that they seem to be able, despite the theories of the *Book of Common Prayer*, to do many good things. The particular boundary on which the NSM thus finds herself is where this shift occurs, a shift not merely in terms of clerical style but much more in terms of what we believe about God and how God is to be discerned. Once again this is where Bonhoeffer found himself:

> 'And we cannot be honest unless we recognize that we have to live in the world *etsi deus non daretur* [even if there were no God]. And this is just what we recognize – before God! God himself compels us to recognize it. So our coming of age leads us to a true recognition of our situation before God. God would have us know that we must live as men who manage our lives without him. The God who is with us is the God who forsakes us (Mark 15.34). The God who lets us live in the world without the working hypothesis of God is the God before whom we stand continually. Before God and with God we live without God. God lets himself be pushed out of the world on to the cross. He is weak and powerless in

the world, and that is precisely the way, the only way, in which he is with us and helps us. Matt. 8.17 makes it quite clear that Christ helps us, not by virtue of his omnipotence, but by virtue of his weakness and suffering.'

(Ibid. pp. 360f)

Many people these days are willing to recognise the idea of the suffering God, the God who enters into our own pain. Indeed in the post-Holocaust, post-Hiroshima world, perhaps no other understanding of God will suffice for humans open to the terrible catastrophes that have characterised the lives of so many. The problem with the idea as it is conventionally used however is that it is predominantly used to minister from weakness to weakness: it most naturally occurs when we are brought face to face with catastrophe, dreadful sickness and death. In such instances it can indeed be potent. Bonhoeffer however is not viewing it thus, for even then it is being used by the Christian as a means of strengthening his position with regard to the weak:

'To be a Christian does not mean to be religious in a particular way, to make something of oneself (a sinner, a penitent, or a saint) on the basis of some method or other, but to be a man – not a type of man, but the man that Christ creates in us. It is not the religious act that makes the Christian, but participation in the sufferings of God in secular life. That is *metanoia*: not in the first place thinking about one's own needs, problems, sins and fears, but allowing oneself to be caught up into the way of Jesus Christ.
 . . . One must completely abandon any attempt to make something of oneself, whether it be a saint, or a converted sinner, or a churchman (a so-called priestly type!), a righteous man or an unrighteous one, a sick one or a health one. By this worldliness I mean living unreservedly in life's duties, problems, successes and failures, experiences and perplexities. In so doing we throw ourselves into the arms of God, taking seriously not our own sufferings, but those of God – watching with Christ in Gethsemane. That, I think, is faith;

that is *metanoia*; and that is how one becomes a man and a Christian.'

(Ibid. pp. 361f, 369f)

Bonhoeffer was writing after the failure of the plot against Hitler, for participation in which he was imprisoned and would later be executed. Very often those to whom his words have been a source of great comfort have been similarly caught up in political and social struggles from a perspective of enormous weakness, those who do not have power or position or prestige, and who recognise in Jesus a fellow struggler.

To be a Christian, to be an ordained minister, is not to be in a position of superiority, but to be a servant. It is perhaps ironical that of all the images used by Jesus of himself, that of servant has tended to be the most neglected and yet could be said to be most representative. We have been called to call no one Father or Teacher (Matthew 23.8–12) yet such commands have repeatedly been ignored and the idea that the clergy exist to serve the people of God not be served by them often remains nothing more than an idea. Ordination is not about elevation. To be a minister in God's world is about having that *metanoia* that will enable us to recognise the goodness of creation and the intrinsic worth of human beings and their achievements, to speak for and with the poorest of God's own longing for a fuller humanity so that the strength of the strong may be shared and enjoyed by all.

But if that answers one question about the way in which our understanding of the Christian doctrine of the human person leads us to see that authentic ministry is from weakness to strength, we must then consider something of what this means in the most practical of ways in terms of what ministers do say of themselves and their God in contexts where there is either apathy or hostility. What does mission mean?

One group of Christians used to meet every Tuesday in an office block in their factory. They came together for Bible study and prayer, to offer each other mutual support. From time to time they used their meetings to discuss ways in which the Christian faith could be made known among their fellow-workers. In the main this meant aligning their actions with church evangelistic campaigns that were going on in their town. On one occasion the Argentinian evangelist Luis Palau was holding a big mission in a nearby city and this group 'targeted' certain of those with whom they worked, in whom they had detected a measure of interest in the church, however small, as those whom they would seek to invite to a meeting, and for whose conversion they prayed.

I was always very impressed by their sense of conviction – most of them were quite open about their Christian faith and wore a lapel badge of some kind or other, and at one level they were certainly seeking to take seriously the command to preach the gospel – or were they? Could not Bonhoeffer say of them that were merely seeking to shore up their own faith by seeking to make more people like themselves? Was it really the gospel they were seeking to propagate or was it religion?

An initiative by another Christian in the same place of work stands in marked contrast. He was concerned about the strong undercurrent of racial mistrust that characterised so much of the life of this particular workplace. So he organised a series of lunchtime meetings over a period of weeks in which men and women of different religious beliefs could have the chance to tell those with whom they worked something of what it is they believe and why they do some things differently. Outside speakers representing Jews, Christians, Hindus, Sikhs and Moslems came and gave a presentation outlining essential aspects of their life and although only about five per cent of the total workforce ever came that was sometimes many more than attended union meetings. So impressed were the management, that together with the site unions they decided to make this initiative a precedent for their own official follow-up meetings.

Although racial mistrust and fear continued it was abundantly clear that this particular initiative was experienced as a means of lessening some of it.

In this second example of mission the Christian was in no way attempting any kind of implicit imperialism, demanding that others were only acceptable if they were like himself. He recognised and valued people of different traditions and beliefs for themselves, recognising that thereby men and women were often able to be more human that they were otherwise, but seeing that ignorance of this served to enhance fear and mistrust. He did not himself feel as a result of his efforts that he wanted to stop being a Christian, but neither did he wish anyone else to stop being what they were.

An interesting spin-off to the second example was that one of those attending was the convenor for one of the site unions – an atheist. He did not feel any particular attraction for any of the religions on offer, but it did make him feel that his own position ought somehow also to be recognised and heard and valued. Although the management were eventually to turn down his suggestion (for fear of the political overtones that would unquestionably have been part of his message) he somehow felt it right that his own atheistic position be legitimately regarded as being just as worthy as others. Perhaps it is worth observing that he and the person whose original initiative the meetings had been were good friends and close colleagues in their political party.

As Jesus might have said: Which of the two Christian groups proved the neighbour to those with whom they worked? A concern for individuals motivated the first group, and any Christian would presumably believe that simply in the interests of truth, it could only be to the advantage of anyone that they come to know something of the love of God revealed in Jesus Christ. The second model, the result of one person's initiative, was also concerned with people coming to know and experience love, but did not feel that it was only validated if it was wearing an obviously Christian label. His concern was for communities and their appropriation of a greater quality of corporate living.

In recounting the stories it will be clear where my own sympathies lie. In thinking about mission, generally and in the most practical of ways as it is of concern to the life of the local church and its ministers, much of my thinking has been shaped by the writings of Max Warren and, to a lesser extent, his successor as General Secretary of the Church Missionary Society, Bishop John Taylor. Both men moved from an evangelical position which gave pride of place in mission to the proclaimed word to a recognition that the commands of the risen Christ to heal, to teach and to proclaim are not necessarily given in a particular order and are not in any kind of opposition to one another. Rather they complement one another as the Church searches out and proclaims the presence of the Kingdom of God.

If God is the God of all the earth, then God is, and always has been present in human communities, including those which reject belief in any kind of god, as well as those whose God is known by names other than those familiar to and beloved of Christians. He is not brought into any place simply because a Christian is present, but wherever men and women have been seeking the cause of humanity so he has been served. When a Christian minister once described his role at work to me as 'being the presence of Jesus in that place' I really felt his words were close to blasphemy, and whenever Christians regard their work as merely a means to an end, the real point of which is serving Jesus in the life of the local church, once again they come near to missing the whole point of what it is that the biblical revelation of a God encountered and served in history, proclaims.

Mission can ever so easily contract into imperialism. In the past this has often been so and it is an ever-present possibility at the present too. It is perhaps always likely to be so when the domains of the Kingdom of God are defined in terms of the domains of the Church – however conceived.

As such it is characterised by a ministering from an alleged position of strength towards a position of alleged inadequacy. It may well be that there are times when a Christian will need to name the source of the hope that is in her (I Peter 3.16) but if ever this is used as a means to power over another there is an intrinsic contradiction between word and content.

As with all lay men and women, the NSM is on the front line of the Church's mission. She is called to be a role model for their own discipleship and, like them, knows the inevitability of the compromises her position will demand. Nevertheless she is called to be alongside God in ministering from weakness to the strength of humans in their communities. Ultimately the only possible account to make any sense of her position will be in terms of the love she manifests, a love worked out and expressed in and through the particular structures of her place of work, the local community or her home. She will know that what matters to God is the quality of living enjoyed by persons in relationship with others. Any and all who recognise that, and like her, live on the boundary between the human and whatever ideology, are her fellow-workers, her brothers and sisters under God, whatever creed they might otherwise profess. At times indeed she will no doubt recognise that only by forswearing any kind of public acknowledgement of her own creed can there be any kind of going forward. At times indeed she will also probably find herself in conflict with those who might share her profession of faith in Christ but with whom, she has otherwise little in common. It is of the nature of standing on the boundary that there will be many who will not, or cannot, see clearly where you are standing and therefore, for their own reasons to doubt, will misunderstand and probably abuse you. Though most NSMs who find themselves thus caught would probably eschew any kind of heroic appellation, their willingness to stand and going on standing is not without enormous value.

CHAPTER SIX

Between the Present and the Future

The figures shown in earlier chapters reveal a fall in the numbers of those presenting themselves for ordination in recent years. To gauge the full significance of this it is necessary to recognise that there are now more clergy retiring than being ordained each year, and that this can only become worse as more and more older men and women are ordained. At my own theological college (long-since closed down) the average age of students must have been under 25 years of age; at the residential college here in Salisbury it is 35 years. Now that retirement with a home is possible for clergy at 65, and more or less compulsory at 70, there is going to come a time before very long when the present crisis will assume very serious proportions.

To many people one answer to this could come from the ordination of women to the priesthood. Were this to go ahead in the mid-1990s (and it begins to look more and more unlikely) it would make available many more priests able to minister where deacons cannot. By itself however it could not solve all the problems now facing the Church, and its opponents would no doubt argue that it will certainly cause many more than it will solve.

Although I recognise the enormous problems of the inner-city Church, from my own experience as a rural incumbent I cannot avoid feeling that it is in rural areas that this is all going to have the most serious consequences. Parishes where formerly there was a resident incumbent have often now been grouped together and it is not unknown for clergy to have the charge of as many as nine or ten parishes. A recently appointed Archbishops' Commission on Rural Areas will no doubt call the attention of the whole Church to this, but realistically what can be done and is there anything that non-stipendiary ministry can contribute? Indeed what might be the possible place of non-stipendiary ministry in the future of the Church and its mission?

One response seems to regard NSMs as potential stipendiary ministers and there is evidence that some NSMs have come under a fair degree of persuasion to 'opt into' parochial ministry and become part of the response of the institution to its crisis. This changeover is becoming a much more familiar event and residential theological colleges are increasingly experiencing NSMs coming into residence for a term before being given a particular parochial charge. In some dioceses even this minor condition of a period in residence is dropped and an NSM may simply be instituted into a living; others have been asked to complete a shortened stipendiary curacy before being given a parish of their own.

There are two main drives to this process. The first is the obvious one of the needs facing the Church, and particularly in rural areas. NSMs are qualified and local and it seems an easy and attractive option for dioceses to make use of them in this way. That operates alongside the other drive which is the willing desire of many NSMs to collude with the dioceses and leave the complexities of seeking somehow to live out a non-stipendiary ministry. Of course some NSMs never particularly wanted a work-based ministry and have come to non-stipendiary ministry precisely because they want to be more involved in parish life in the belief that any ministry they might have is firmly focussed upon the life of the local church. Given the fall in numbers their hopes for yet greater involvement in the ecclesiastical machine is likely to be realised. Although complete figures for the number of people 'switching' from NSM to stipendiary are not available, it is clearly somewhere in the region of a third of those who have spent time working as an NSM.

Even if actual stipendiary ministry is not possible (and many practicalities could make this so) other NSMs are more than happy to give more and more of their time to working as if they were stipendiary and accept the invitations of hard-pressed rural deans and archdeacons to cover a parish during an interregnum.

Using NSMs as some kind of stop-gap would seem to me regrettable in the extreme. First of all, it is colluding with the understandable desire that some NSMs have of avoiding the complexities and tensions of living on the boundaries with which I have been concerned throughout this book. At stake in that issue is not merely one of personal preference but a whole way of thinking about what ministry is and might be in the world today. Second, it is using NSMs as some kind of elastoplast stuck over a gaping hole; in no way does it address the real crisis we face, nor adequately assess the creative possibilities that may well be inherent in it and in particular with regard to lay ministry.

Perhaps the central issue with which the Church as a whole has to come to terms in planning for the future and facing its present crisis is the reality of God. To what extent do we as a Church regard ourselves as being in a living relationship with and dependent upon the God encountered within the circumstances of human being and becoming? As with Israel, the Church is inevitably likely to find change difficult, but what if God is present in the change? What if the collapse of the institutional Church is itself part of the process whereby God is renewing his people for the service of his Kingdom?

Few people would have the courage to say with their hand on their heart that the Church as it is adequately represents the God manifest in Jesus Christ. The Church must always be the becoming Church, ever in need of reform, so that it may complete its vocation to be like John the Baptist, the one that points away from itself to the Christ and his Kingdom and its demands.

The trouble with the innate conservatism of an institution like the Church of England is that it cannot see how the future will not look exactly like the past. Engaging in recruitment drives so as to make the continuation of the past possible has thus become the order of the day, and part of that, at least, is the attempt to persuade more NSMs into stipendiary ministry.

But perhaps God does not want the future to be a replica of the past (not least for the very good reason that the past was far from glorious and is, in part, responsible for the present crisis). This is not to say that there is no place for the ordained ministry. For a number of reasons I am convinced that there is, but there is also an important place for other ministries, and even more important than all this there is the reality of the Kingdom of God, God's active present ruling, which is the reason for which there exists a Church in the first place. We do not create the Kingdom, God alone can do that; we exist merely to proclaim and serve it, and the sooner we can begin to shape our structures to this end, the sooner we shall be able to do justice to what it is we actually believe.

Mission begins with the realisation that God is the God of all the earth, ever-present and willing the bringing together of creation with himself, the work for which Christ was born. The Church is called by God to be the vehicle of his summons to human beings and the vanguard of those who work together with God towards unity and love.

The ordained clergy exist to further the possibility of the Church being able to fulfil its vocation. They are to do this by their own example and by their teaching and by their support of the other 'lay' Christians. Non-stipendiary clergy can do some of these things better than their stipendiary colleagues; in others the time available to stipendiaries will make possible things less accessible to NSMs. After all there is work needing to be done which requires availability: buildings needing to be maintained (increasingly a crippling burden of the rural Church); the diaconal work of visiting the housebound and liasing with secular agencies similarly engaged; there is teaching to be prepared; all these and other tasks will continue to require men and women who have the time to enable them to happen.

Other tasks, such as those of building up the life of the community through visiting and sharing experience, leading the community in prayer and worship, focussing the community in its dealings with other groups and being the visible example of a person engaged with God and the demands of his Kingdom can be done as well by a non-stipendiary as they can by a stipendiary minister. And in rural communities where there is a powerful case as ever there was for the visible presence of a representative person, one way forward would be the ordination of more non-stipendiary ministers, not turning those we already have into stipendiaries. This might be approached in two ways.

The first would be to seek to encourage and support NSMs to move into communities in which they would be acting as a non-stipendiary incumbent. This would of course necessitate the Church being involved in helping with the costs of buying and selling a house, for those willing to move in this way must not be made to bear the financial cost themselves. Of course in some places the Church still owns property and it might be possible for NSMs to move into former parsonage houses. In others, where the house has been sold, the NSM would have to sell their existing house and buy property in the new community, in which process the Church should be willing to give some support, perhaps through no-interest bridging loans. Once the house has been bought by the NSM the diocese would have no further responsibility for its upkeep.

In fact such a pattern is already happening in one or two places and proving enormously valuable. For not only is such a pattern of operation possible, it is also enabling the local church to realise their own responsibilities for those things which formerly they might have left to the vicar. They still have an incumbent who provides the community with leadership and support, plus the ability to speak to them from the context of his own work with all its compromises and demands on his time, but they also know that to maintain this situation they have to play their own part and recognise that they too are ministers. In such a community the retired and those with time during the day have begun to see how they can be positively active fulfilling their own calling and at the same time enabling the Church thereby to be the Church in their community. Lay people can visit the sick, can take the reserved sacrament to the housebound, can attend to the needs of the church building, and, with appropriate training, lead Bible studies and discussions. Indeed for many people the opportunity to do these things brings with it a sense of fulfilment of their own vocational longings.

So this may well be one way in which the Church can begin to make better use of its non-stipendiary ministers. Unfortunately it has limited possibilities. The rural dioceses where there are fewer clergy tend also to be the dioceses where there are fewer NSMs because they are also the dioceses with lower populations. NSMs in secular employment need to be within reach of their employment and the far reaches of the diocese of Norwich, for example, do not lend them-selves to easy travel by any mode! So whilst this may well be something deserving of considerable thought in some in-stances, other solutions need to be sought and in this something positive might well be offered by the further development of Local Non-Stipendiary Ministry.

All the anxieties aroused by the idea of NSM such as the loss of professionalism and status of the clergy, are height-ened by the idea of LNSM. Ordaining men and women in local communities as priests and deacons, without expect-ing of them the training and assessment demanded by stipendiary and non-stipendiary courses, giving them a local licence so that they only operate within clear and definite boundaries; all this presents many problems to church people and especially to many clergy.

Yet the possibilities are enormous. Ordaining a natural leader of a community so that he or she becomes the clear representative person of the Church has a great deal to say for itself in terms of theology. If God is encountered within the life of a community, so a community needs to take some responsibility for its response to God. Asking a community to take the responsibility of selecting from its number someone to lead it, to represent it, to support and encourage it, but not to behave in a 'clerical' way, aping the patterns of the past, could be said to correspond to the sort of choices made by the communities in the Acts of the Apostles. It would give to the local church an autonomy which would represent a proper balance to the authority of the wider Church which of course alone has the power to ordain someone presented as a candidate. There would of course need to be training, but why would it be necessary for such training to be exactly like the patterns of training that have traditionally characterised preparation for ordination? New patterns of training, experientially based, rooted in each diocese and relying heavily on the life and experience of the local church could provide exactly what men and women would need to enable them to do the particular task laid upon them. But that task would not be the same as they previously saw being performed by their former 'Rector'. Such LNSMs would not be incumbents, and indeed a whole new way of thinking and working would be needed to begin to do justice to the practice of such a vision. Rural Deans would perhaps be more like bishops, exercising a proper ministry of episcopacy: oversight, in relation to the work of a number of local priests and deacons.

Of course there are a good many problems which need to be faced before this can become a greater reality, though in some dioceses, e.g. Lincoln, this is already becoming a familiar part of diocesan life. Quite what it means to ordain a person to a limited ministry when traditionally ordination has been seen as becoming part of something wider is just one of the problems that urgently requires attention. If the past is regarded as being the only possible model, it will be extremely difficult to take LNSM forward but if the present crisis now facing the Church can be seen as the moment of opportunity then various forms of NSM may well have a huge part to play in the way the Church responds positively to the opportunities being presented to it by God.

Part of the way in which the future is being addressed is a major rethink about the pattern and shape of training for the non-stipendiary ministry. At the present time training is based upon a network of courses which have more or less sprung up spontaneously so that dioceses have been able to send their particular candidates to the nearest. Some of these are proving expensive to run, others seem to have too few candidates to do proper justice to the educational needs of their students. At long last the bishops have begun to consider ways in which the training for NSM can be best shaped. Clearly it may well look somewhat different in three or four years time.

At the moment there are three basic models in use. One, such as that used by the Southwark Ordination Course, is geared to the needs of those who live, more or less, within the boundaries of Greater London and who can manage to come together on two weekday evenings in the centre of London for lectures and seminars. On top of this there are seven residential weekends and a nine-day summer school for each student in each year of a three-year course. Quite a number of other courses, especially those with large urban centres use this model of training. The Northern Ordination Course for example, which covers a massive area in the north of England provides evening sessions in three different urban centres: Manchester, Liverpool and Leeds, and relies heavily on the motorway network for student travelling.

A second model, such as that used in the St Albans Diocese Ministerial Training Scheme, seeks to combine ordination training with training for the whole Church in a most imaginative and far-sighted way. Most candidates come on the course prior to selection and during the first part of the course an essential element of the training is concerned with seeking to clarify and discern precisely what sort of ministry best suits which people. Some then go to an

ACCM Selection Conference and others do not, preparing for a variety of accredited lay ministries in the diocese. Throughout, the training of lay and ordained ministers goes on in harmony, an attempt to clarify the real partnership which ought to characterise all ministry. Students attend a local centre twice weekly in term time for lectures and seminars and there are five residential weekends and a summer school each year in addition.

The third model, such as that used by the course for which I work, is able to cover an extensive geographical area because it does not rely on students coming to a particular centre during the week. The educational approach of the course utilises written material on which students work at home and at a weekly meeting with a local tutor. This is supplemented by five residential weekends and a summer school in each of the three years of training. The educational material has been written with the particular needs of this form of training in mind, and local tutors and incumbents of students receive guidance and support in their work with students. Because of the low travelling costs it is cheaper than some other forms of training and because it makes use of local tutors is flexible enough to be able to cope with fluctuations in numbers and location of students. It is particularly useful when large distances are being covered and appeals to students whose work commitments would not allow them two evenings a week based in a particular urban centre.

Quite what the shape of training will be at the end of the process of re-thinking is not at the moment clear, though cost-effectiveness will almost certainly mean some of the present courses will have to change, and maybe even disappear. On top of that the further development of LNSM will probably become a major influence in the further development of patterns. It is certainly very much to be hoped that decisions can be made not just on the basis of cost and that somehow or other the possibilities arising from NSM together with the training needs of the whole

Church can be considered as the next stage of training is thought about and eventually engineered. As Bishop John Taylor wrote during his time as Bishop of Winchester in the light of his experience of one particular course:

> 'If NSM training is not earthed in lay secular experience, if it is not wrestling with the questions which that experience has raised, if it is not trying to address the complex issues raised by the world of work and the problems of our society and of what it means to be a Christian in the world, then without realising it NSMs will increasingly be dominated by the questions and demands not of the world but of the institutionalised church. NSMs will lose their distinctive vocation of being on the boundaries of both the church and the world and of helping each to listen and to tell their story to the other. The future surely demands that we work out ways in which laity are included as a matter of course in the training of their clergy'

(Fuller 1984, p. 94)

The future of the Church then may well look quite different from what it has at various times in the past. In fact of course there is no 'final' form of the Church, it has always had to adapt to the circumstances in which it is set and the contexts in which it is to fulfil its vocation. What is unchanging is the vocation, the call to proclaim through its words and common life the God revealed in Jesus Christ, the creator and ruler of all, who wills the unity of all creation, and whose work is to bring it about (c.f. Colossians 1.15–20).

The central concern of this book however lies in the belief that we attend to this vocation not by engaging in constant ecclesiastical machination and revision but by being outward facing, engaging with the world as the locus of the divine activity. The non-stipendiary ordained minister has a marvellous opportunity to be in the vanguard of this work of the Church and to be a leader of those many other 'lay' Christians who find themselves on the front line of mission. But it does mean being willing to stand and to go on standing on the boundaries, painful and complex though that will be at various times, because that is where the action is and where Christ must be proclaimed.

For myself one of the images that has most helped focus my understanding of such a ministry comes from Shakespeare. I much lament the fact that during the revision of the Church's calendar no place was found for him. Of the English poets George Herbert alone is included (unless one also counts Keble). John Donne is another mysteriously omitted. His poetry is arguably finer than Herbert's and his ministry longer, but perhaps his love poetry is held against him! As for Shakespeare, it would not be his piety for which I would have commemorated (of which I know nothing), but because anyone who can reveal the workings of the human heart, as he does, must be worth commemorating among the human greats.

For more than fifteen years now I have been fascinated by Shakespeare's fools. From Touchstone to Feste and on to the crowning glory of Lear's fool we are offered something quite astonishing, a world transformed by true vision. Shakespeare relied heavily for his inspiration for these parts on the actor for whom they were created, Robert Armyne. Born in 1568 he was first apprenticed as a goldsmith but revealed such talents as an extempore stage wit and popular pamphleteer that he entered Shakespeare's company where he unquestionably exerted a considerable influence upon the parts which Shakespeare wrote for him.

Perhaps the first thing which audiences would have noted of Armyne's creation of his master's fools were the clothes he wore for the part. Abandoning the traditional cap and bells, he elected to don 'motley', the name used for the long overcoat worn by the mentally subnormal and, thus attired, set about the transformation of the medieval clown-jester, much beloved of audiences, into that of the idiot. This was first seen in the part of Lavatch, written for him in *All's Well That Ends Well*, where he is afforded the traditional licence of the mentally ill of speaking *cum privilegio*, a licence somewhat akin to parliamentary privilege. His next part was that of Touchstone in *As You Like It* where the fool is the 'touchstone' of what is true and false (though also no doubt in part a pun on the fact that a touchstone was a vital part of the equipment of Armyne's own profession of goldsmith). It was in *Twelfth Night* however that we first see the fully developed idiot-fool, Feste, happy, as his name suggests – yet:

> 'This fellow is wise enough to play the fool;
> And to do that craves a kind of wit:
> He must observe their mood on whom he jests,
> And, like the haggard, check at every feather
> That comes before his eye. This is a practice
> As full of labour as a wise man's art . . .'

(Act 3 Scene 1)

Yet the crowning jewel of his achievement is the fool of *King Lear*, where clothed in the mantle of a common idiot he assumes the proportions of a Greek Chorus as the only one able to recognise the true dimensions of the unfolding tragedy.

He wrote a book about folly called *Foole upon Foole*, based upon visits he had made to asylums for the mentally insane, and Shakespeare shows clear evidence of having drawn deeply upon this work. With great sensitivity and compassion Armyne explores the world of madness and inner darkness, reflecting an awareness of the place of such within the divine economy in such a way as immediately recalls the later Caroline divines and poets. It is little wonder that one of the great twentieth century writers on the history of the fool in literature, Enid Welsford, maintained that Shakespeare's fools often manifest the ethics 'of the New Testament . . . the reiteration of the wilder paradoxes and St Paul'. What we are offered in the vision of Robert Armyne allied to the genius of Shakespeare is a vision of a world turned upside down, where the first are last, and the last unquestionably first, and where the truly weak speak truly to the powerful and strong.

If we are serious about looking for the vision necessary to sustain non-stipendiary ministry, a ministry on the boundary, then I believe we could do a lot worse than to look at the fools of Shakespeare as our models.

St John Chrysostom once wrote that the chief reason why the Church revered the apostle Paul was for his folly for the sake of the gospel. Certainly in the first letter to the Corinthians Paul sets out the paradox of the cross as the chief manifestation of God, a complete overturning of human wisdom and the revelation of a folly wiser than the wise. On this foundation he came as a minister among them, earning his living by manual craft and from a position of weakness proclaiming a God revealed in weakness he set about transforming the world.

Shakespeare's fools are never the principal actors in the drama, indeed for their pains they are often assumed to be there to be the butt of other people's jokes. Their essential role is determined less by what they do than by what they are, though what they are often has powerful consequences for the action of the play. They are available and accessible, where people are, ready when occasion demands just to listen and comfort, at other times to lead the revels or, on occasion, be the one who can interpret what is happening and give expression to it. Sometimes, though rarely, they are even drawn into activity (as with Feste and his attempts to bring Malvolio down a peg or two). Perhaps most powerfully they are the ones who have to sit and endure the pain of recognising the truth but being quite unable to do anything other than live in the face of the most appalling catastrophe, to recognise and name it for what it is, and go on living with it.

NSMs, like other clergy know what it is to be teased and mocked and even humiliated – this is not an easy time for the Christian faith. In this respect they are bound to share something of the fate of the 'fools for Christ' of Eastern

Orthodoxy, men and women who recognised that their public confession of faith would bring them the mockery of others – as it did Paul. They too in their unusual ministry are characterised less by what they do – hardly any obviously clerical functions – than by what they are, which is to say, men and women who publicly represent the Church, publicly represent God. Like the fools they do not wait for others to come to them but are to be found in the market place, where people gather, where people are at ease and in charge of their lives. In their work, in the community, in the home they are there to listen and comfort, at times they take their share in the celebrations of the workplace and community (not because of any 'special' or privileged role which is sometimes accorded the vicar) but because they genuinely belong there. At times too they will be the one who sets change in motion in the pursuit of the Kingdom of God and its demands of righteousness, at others they will be there to interpret and understand and lament when the realities of the workplace damage and hurt others. Above all they continue to be there, not merely being involved at special moments or when major crises demand major interventions (something which characterises so much parochial ministry) but there afterwards when others have forgotten and put the hard things out of mind. Then their ministry is expressed above all through their persistence and willingness to endure inactivity.

So what is needed in the NSMs of the future? I believe the first requirement is a faith rooted in the biblical witness to the God who was encountered by Israel in the vagaries of national and international life; the God who met Joseph in the complexities of Egyptian political life; whom Moses sought to serve through the complexities of the legal system; whom David met on the field of battle; whom the prophets knew had to be served not merely in the temple but in the practicalities of justice and honesty; whom the second Isaiah recognised in the actions of a Persian king; who was made known through the pregnancy of a young unmarried girl in the tiny village of Nazareth; who was seen and touched and known on a gallows, a man executed on a political charge. This is the God to whom the Bible witnesses. The great theologian Karl Barth said of a faith in such a God that prayer was characterised by holding the Bible in one hand and today's newspaper in the other – a faith that believes that God is met in his world and has to be responded to there, however apparently secular. It is a faith that knows that at its centre lies nothing that we do in the way of religion, but all that God is doing, and in which work we are called, all humanity, to share as the Kingdom is brought to its fullness.

To this must be added a willingness, and an accompanying openness, to share this vision and faith with others, to strengthen and build up the whole people of God. That will require enormous sensitivity to the differences between human beings and one of the great advantages of non-residential training (with one exception – that based at Oak Hill College in London caters almost exclusively for evangelical students) is that it brings together people of widely differing churchmanships and offers them an opportunity to learn why and how people see things in different ways to themselves. To be willing to lead the Church is above all a willingness to listen and learn and share something of themselves, as well as accepting the responsibilities of being a public person, a public representative of God and the Church, and consequently, a person who will be looked at, and to, by others, often critically, often for a lead and inspiration.

The third requirement must be a profound respect for the whole of creation as God's creation, and above all for the men and women who are made in the image and likeness of God, many of whom show many more signs of being such than some of those who come to church, and with whom we work as fellow workers in the cause of that which is human. Being a Christian, being an ordained minister of the Church – neither of these have anything to do with being superior to others. God has after all made us human before any of us become Christian. Becoming more human ought to be the first work in which we are engaged; perhaps when we have achieved that we can then think about becoming Christian!

A faith in a living God who is not limited to the boundaries of religion, a recognition that the Church is nothing more than a means to an end, and the call to become more human – these three represent the heart of what any prospective ordinand requires. To these, for an NSM, must be added a willingness to live it out within the particular circumstances of the life already being lived. It is not about going somewhere else to find security in a role and a structure that caters to your needs, but being and serving where you are now. It is not easy – but for the sake of the Kingdom of God, it is there on the boundary that they are called to be.

FOR FURTHER READING

Mark Hodge: *Non-Stipendiary Ministry in the Church of England* (CIO Publishing) 1983
Edd. Baelz & Jacob: *Ministers of the Kingdom* (CIO 1985)
Ed. John Fuller, SDMTS: *A Model of a Training Scheme* (Published by Salisbury & Wells Theological College 1984)
Edd. Fuller & Vaughan: *Working For The Kingdom* (SPCK 1986)
Peter Selby: *Look For The Living* (SCM 1976)
Ordination Training On Courses (ACCM 1989)
John V. Taylor: *Kingdom Come* (SCM 1989)
Monica Furlong: *Mirror To The Church* (SPCK 1988)